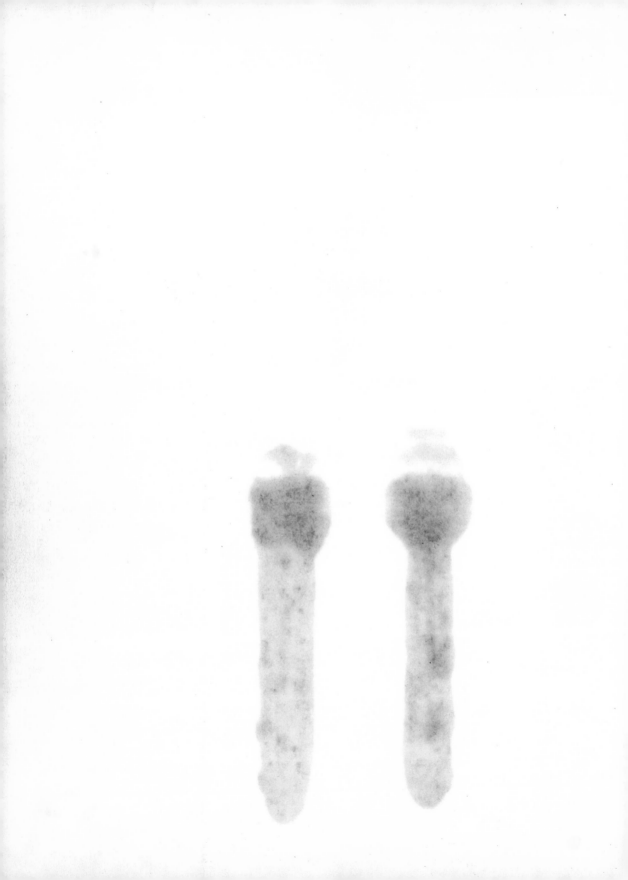

Homebuilt Aircraft

Homebuilt Aircraft

David B. Thurston

Consulting Aeronautical Engineer
President, Thurston Aeromarine Corporation

McGraw-Hill Book Company

New York   St. Louis   San Francisco   Auckland   Bogotá   Hamburg
Johannesburg   London   Madrid   Mexico   Montreal   New Delhi
Panama   Paris   São Paulo   Singapore   Sydney   Tokyo   Toronto

Library of Congress Cataloging in Publication Data

Thurston, David B
   Homebuilt aircraft.

   (McGraw-Hill series in aviation)
   Includes index.
   1. Airplanes, Homebuilt. I. Title.
TL671.2.T58   629.133'3   80-26416
ISBN 0-07-064552-3

1234567890   VHVH   898765432

The editors for this book were Jeremy Robinson and Christine M. Ulwick, the designer was Mark E. Safran, and the production supervisor was Thomas G. Kowalczyk. It was set in Optima by David Seham Associates, Inc.

Printed and bound by Von Hoffmann Press, Inc.

Jacket photo: A Pitts Special chasing a Hawaiian rainbow. *(John W. Underwood.)*
Front endpaper: The Marguart MA-5 two-place Charger biplane at Oshkosh.
Back endpaper: The custom designed Sprinter received an award at Oshkosh '79.
All designs and specifications of aircraft courtesy of the designers.
All photos by David B. Thurston, unless otherwise noted.
Art for part opening pages executed by Carl U. Burch.

McGraw-Hill Series in Aviation

David B. Thurston, Consulting Editor

Ramsey *Budget Flying* (1981)
Sacchi *Ocean Flying* (1979)
Smith *Aircraft Piston Engines* (1981)
Thomas *Personal Aircraft Maintenance* (1981)
Thurston *Design for Flying* (1978)
Thurston *Design for Safety* (1980)
Thurston *Homebuilt Aircraft* (1982)

About the Author

DAVID B. THURSTON earned an aeronautical engineering degree from New York University's Guggenheim School of Aeronautics, and received the Chance Vought Award for his senior year aircraft design project. Since that time he has been associated with the design of sixteen aircraft including the Brewster Buffalo fighter; various Grumman aircraft such as the F6F Hellcat, F9F Panther, and F11F Tigercat; the supersonic Rigel missile; and three light planes developed for Mr. Roy Grumman.

More recently, Mr. Thurston has concentrated on the personal aircraft field, designing the Colonial Skimmer, predecessor of the Lake Buccaneer Amphibian, the small Teal Amphibian, the four-place Trojan Amphibian, and the high-performance Sequoia aerobatic landplane. His research on aircraft hydro-ski and hydrofoil development resulted in his writing a manual of hydrofoil seaplane design for the U. S. Navy.

Mr. Thurston heads his own aircraft design consulting firm, Thurston Aeromarine Corporation, and is an active private pilot holding a current instrument rating. He is the author of *Design for Flying* (1978) and *Design for Safety* (1980).

To the many homebuilders whose enthusiasm and perseverance overcome the obstacles of toil and time.

Contents

Preface   xiii
Introduction   3

The beginning of homebuilding
Number of homebuilt aircraft
Commitment of time and money required
Scope of text

Part One The Homebuilt Movement

1. Why Homebuilt Aircraft   5

Three basic groups of builders
The EAA and Oshkosh
Satisfaction and reasons for building
Airplane selection
Time and cost considerations
The continuing hobby of building

2. Homebuilder Profiles   11

General background requirements
The need for perseverance, self-discipline, and organization
Extent of family support
Building to relax
Preferred type of construction
Effort required
Social aspects of homebuilding

3. Extent of the Movement   15

Dollar volume
Active organizations
Experimental Aircraft Association

National Association of Sport Aircraft Designers
Pioneer, World War I, antique, and classic periods
Aerobatic activity
Ultralight aircraft

4. Homebuilt Safety   23

EAA designees and forums
Materials substitution procedures
Number of aircraft under construction
The need for flight proficiency
A safety record similar to production aircraft
Safety procedures

Part Two Aircraft Available

5. Designs and Designers   29

Variety of aircraft offered
Types of construction
Design selection criteria
Assembly space available
Configuration and performance characteristics
Seating capacity
Fabricated parts and kits
Powerplant selection
Airport availability
Handling qualities
Designer's reputation

6. Builder's Choice — Airplanes Galore   39

Three-view drawings, dimensional data, performance values, and
brief background for landplanes, helicopters, sailplanes and
gliders (including powered types), seaplanes, and ultralights

7. Pioneer, Antique, Classic, Replica, and Custom
Aircraft   139

Antique and classic restoration
Pioneer and World War I replicas
Sources for old plans
Replica sources and data for eight aircraft
The saga of Schatzie, a custom airplane

8. Powerplant Selection   153

Certified versus conversion engines
Certified models and aircraft using them, Continental and Lycoming
Uncertified types available; installation references

Part Three Materials and Methods

9. Shop Requirements   173

Working space
Positioning shop tools
Fold-brake design
Sources for aircraft tools
Shop technique and construction references

10. Materials, Processes, and Finishes   179

Materials specifications, strength values, and hardness tables
Alclad sheet aluminum alloy
Extrusions
4130 steel
Isolating dissimilar materials
Heat treatment specifications
Working aluminum alloy
Fuel, oil, and hydraulic joint sealing specifications
Alodine finish materials
Wash primer
Surface fillers and finishes
Fiber-glass repairs
Seaplane protection
Sources for aircraft hardware and materials

Part Four Flying and Maintenance Considerations

11. Homebuilder Insurance   195

Why liability and hull coverage
Homebuilt insurance— Avemco and EAA
Determining insurability before selecting a design

12. Those First Flights   197

The first preflight check list
Selecting a pilot for the first flight
Using a parachute and shoulder harness
The importance of cylinder-head temperature
FAA flight restrictions

13. Keeping Airworthy   203

Safety forums
Flying time to remain proficient
Importance of preflight inspection
FAA permission to maintain and inspect your own airplane
How to apply for repairman certificate

Index   205

Preface

Aviation, which was basically a worldwide cottage industry through 1915, has grown into a major and essential technology employing hundreds of thousands of people. Along the way interest has recently turned full cycle for many aviation enthusiasts and sport-flying pilots; we now find that increased leisure time, coupled with the ever-rising cost of small-production airplanes, has developed another aviation-oriented cottage industry—and one that is rapidly assuming the proportions of a big business—homebuilt aircraft.

According to the Experimental Aircraft Association (EAA), one of the leading forces in maintaining and sustaining homebuilder interest, latest estimates of annual sales volume for homebuilt aircraft plans, kits, related parts, and accessories exceed $35 million. With over 60,000 active members receiving the monthly publication *Sport Aviation,* the EAA Annual Convention at Oshkosh, Wisconsin, regularly draws over 400,000 of the faithful during an 8-day period ending the first week of August.

The Federal Aviation Administration (FAA) has cooperated with homebuilders to provide field inspection supervision and construction suggestions that assist in keeping homebuilt safety levels similar to those for certified production aircraft. And the FAA is to be commended for this interest even though their participation may occasionally seem restrictive or time-consuming; flight safety is the essential goal, so FAA regulations are necessary for every builder's personal protection.

The homebuilt safety record also speaks well for the designers of these aircraft, many of whom work from intuition and experience rather than a formal engineering education. But it is results that count, and that is really what this book is all about: the homebuilders and designers and their airplanes, construction, and aircraft operating procedures. In short, it is about the why and how of the modern homebuilt movement.

Along the way, much assistance was provided by many designers and builders who kindly supplied specifications and photographs of their best creative efforts. I am deeply indebted to these people because designers are frequently reluctant to reveal their secrets, and this book could not have been written without their cooperation.

Over 100 different homebuilt aircraft are reviewed in some detail—including three-view drawings, specifications, and photos. A few worthy aircraft have not been included because several requests for data remained unanswered, while a few available designs have not been presented simply because I consider them either too difficult to fly or too flimsy for safe operation.

Credit is due the various suppliers of tools and materials source information who served to make this book a more useful reference manual. One of the great problems faced by all homebuilders is that of finding a particular part, tool, or item of raw material; in fact, building one's own airplane frequently seems to be more of a correspondence effort than a construction problem. The volume of paperwork gradually becomes enormous, although this book should considerably reduce such burdensome expenditures of time.

I would also like to express my appreciation to Tom Poberezny, executive vice president of the Experimental Aircraft Association, for the special background information he supplied; to our older son, Kent Thurston, for his excellent photographic support in preparing my homebuilt photos for reproduction; and again to my wife, Evelyn, for her editorial comment and typing effort in translating my writing into a manuscript. As a last, but by no means least, note of appreciation, we all owe a debt of gratitude to the many volunteers who keep homebuilt aircraft interest alive, safe, and growing all over the world.

David B. Thurston

The Homebuilt Movement

Introduction

HOMEBUILT AIRCRAFT

With a project under way that requires at least 1 year and, more likely, 3 to 7 years of spare-time effort, no one is as eager to save time as the person completing a home-built airplane. And no group is as satisfying to work with as a gathering of home-builders assembling their airplanes piece by piece. There are hundreds of parts per airplane, and each of them must be transferred from detail drawings into a working pattern or tool, then into an actual formed piece, and eventually fastened into place somewhere in the structure. The enormity of the undertaking—even for a very simple airplane—is obvious, and it is no wonder that any and all help and guidance are most welcome and received with appreciation.

Homebuilt Aircraft has been written to describe the homebuilt movement as well as to assist builders and potential builders in selecting a design suitable for their needs. Along the way, we discuss construction methods, list proven sources for essential materials and tools, and describe basic flight-test and maintenance procedures. As a result, this book is a basic reference for homebuilt aircraft construction and operation and a time-saver as well.

In view of the background material and current homebuilding effort covered in some detail, *Homebuilt Aircraft* will also appeal to readers interested in aviation development and the expansion of homebuilt activity.

How did homebuilding begin? Why does it continue to grow? What purpose does it serve? In a real sense, homebuilding has always existed within the framework of the aircraft industry. The pioneers had no manufacturer to turn to, and so they built their prototypes in nearby barns or available vacant buildings. A classic example is the Wright brothers' construction of their Flyers in Dayton, Ohio, and then transporting them to Kitty Hawk, North Carolina, for flight-test work. Bleriot built his own aircraft; so did Curtiss, the Farmans, and others.

As the industry matured, very little surplus capital was accumulated for experimental development. With the exception of research and speed-record aircraft supported by government funds, experimental design concepts or private racing aircraft therefore became the product of small groups organized with limited funds to meet specialized goals. These groups were essentially homebuilders. The original Cessna,

Ryan, Beech, Granville Brothers (GB), Howard and Laird racers, and similar aircraft arose from such humble sources.

Speeds are so high today that it is virtually impossible for small groups to personally fund the design and construction of speed-record and racing aircraft. But at the other end of the spectrum, personal flying is dominated by aircraft derived from the same basic Federal Aviation Administration (FAA) specification, Federal Air Regulation (FAR) Part 23. Anyone wishing a specialized or conceptually different airplane must either design and build one of his or her own or buy a set of flight-tested plans that satisfy their requirements and then construct "the" airplane accordingly. Frequently, the design becomes a bit modified in the process, thus becoming a one-of-a-kind homebuilt and consequently a priceless jewel in the builder's eye. I've seen homebuilts on display where the builder or a helper stands nearby with a soft cloth, ready to remove any fingerprints left by admirers of the art.

With the price of production aircraft continually rising, the number of homebuilt aircraft is growing at a rapid rate—from the 10,000 estimated to be under construction or completed in 1970 to over 20,000 in 1980 (excluding ultralight aircraft). This growth continues to accelerate as more aircraft plans, kits, and parts are made available to fill the demand for all levels of construction and operating performance.

Because of the extraordinary personal commitment required to build one's own airplane, many enthusiasts become discouraged early in the game. While I do not agree with the often-heard remark that "a boat is a hole in the water into which money is poured," there is no doubt that the homebuilt airplane becomes an invader which consumes time, living space, and much available capital. Yet, for the persevering, the eventual first flight makes it all worthwhile.

Homebuilt Aircraft surveys the many aircraft designs offered to homebuilders with due consideration for the handling requirements, cost, and construction complexity of the various models. Parts fabrication and assembly procedures, tooling, material and equipment sources, finishing, flight testing, and desirable levels of pilot competence are also covered in order to provide background *prior* to the jump into a homebuilt program as well as to make life a bit easier *after* the decision has been made and construction is under way.

Building your own airplane becomes a full-time hobby producing a useful end product that provides personal enjoyment for many years; *Homebuilt Aircraft* will shorten the path to this goal. Let us begin by reviewing the homebuilt movement and what it is all about.

Why Homebuilt Aircraft

Despite the fact that about halfway through construction most builders wonder how they became involved in such an all-consuming project, homebuilt aircraft are assembled for almost as many different reasons as there are builders. However, builders seem to break down into three major groups: (1) those primarily interested in building a complex assembly and doing so with great skill, (2) pilots who want to know every part of a special type of airplane so they may personally maintain as well as fly their creation, and (3) those who want to fly but cannot, or do not want to, pay the price of a production airplane.

While not all builders are members of the Experimental Aircraft Association (EAA), this organization serves as a focal point for homebuilt aircraft development and interest. Each year the EAA organizes and sponsors the world's largest airplane meet: the Annual International Convention and Sport Aviation Exhibition or, as it is better known, "Oshkosh." Beginning the end of July or the first days of August at Whitman Field in Oshkosh, Wisconsin, displays of individually styled aircraft, design forums, builders' meetings, and gigantic daily air shows featuring World War II aircraft and aerobatic performances draw over 400,000 visitors during an 8-day period (see Fig. 1-1). Hotel accommodations are regularly reserved a year in advance—and over 8000 homebuilt and production aircraft may be seen on the field during the first weekend of the convention. This largest gathering of airplanes in the world is a result of the organizational ability of the EAA staff and volunteers combined with the unbounded enthusiasm of the thousands of people who build aircraft in their garages, barns, basements, apartments, and, yes, even in their living rooms.

There are two large billboards located in the main foot-traffic area at Oshkosh, right where everyone passes by to attend forums and construction demonstrations and to find lunch. These boards, placed by the EAA to serve as swap spots during the convention, are always filled with notices and snapshots of aircraft for sale, projects and parts available, and so on.

Standing in front of one of these centers of activity for an hour or so while talking with fellow enthusiasts provides exposure to an entire cross section of homebuilding interests. Builders are always ready to exchange experiences, pull out photos of their pride and joy, and discuss their reasons for building.

Figure 1-1   Sixteen AT-6s and SNJs trailed by three Beech T-34s fly by in a multiple diamond formation during the Oshkosh '79 daily air show.

Many craftsmen seek the challenge of working with different construction techniques and materials. Building an airplane can certainly satisfy that need because it necessitates working with steel and aluminum alloys, fabric, and wood; using various assembly processes, such as riveting and welding; as well as different finishes, equipment installation requirements, engine operations, and so on. For many homebuilders, this is the *only* reason for assembling an airplane. A number of obviously capable mechanics have told me quite frankly that they were not pilots, were only completing an airplane because building was their hobby, and that they intended to sell the airplane when completed. In fact, one builder told me he was in the process of completing his sixth airplane and had never flown any of them.

These are members of our first group, and their ages span a range from young people who build and sell aircraft for pleasure or additional income to retired mechanics who wish to remain active doing something they enjoy. Many of them are custom builders, assembling the more complex aerobatic designs such as the Pitts Special, Sequoia S300, Christen Eagle, and similar aircraft for pilots who require special performance, equipment, and finishes for their airplane. However, most members of this group are amateur builders devoting their spare hours to this hobby for a variety of reasons ranging from escapism or relaxing therapy (as long as all goes well) to sheer enjoyment of building something well—particularly if it can fly!

Our second group probably includes the greatest number of builders of heavier, powered aircraft; heavier, that is, than ultralight gliders and powered sailplanes. This group includes pilots who are handy, like to build, and enjoy owning an airplane. Many builders in this group could easily afford to purchase a certified production model, but they prefer to fly a unique or custom type of airplane they can point to with that special pride associated with building one's own airplane. Probably most builders in this group construct airplanes because they enjoy sport flying and building an airplane of their own is the only way to fly the type of airplane desired. These pilots know there is nothing comparable to flying cross-country in the open cockpit of a monoplane or biplane on a spring day; and if they must build an airplane to get up there, so be it! As an added bonus, being thoroughly familiar with the entire ship assures and simplifies proper maintenance by the owner, thus providing the dual benefits of increased safety and lower flying cost.

But many would-be pilots and pilots who lack the funds to fly are not at all interested in spending 2 to 7 years constructing an airplane. These people constitute the third group of homebuilders, and are, to a large degree, responsible for the explosive growth of ultralight aircraft, a type of simplified airplane frequently weighing little more than the pilot strapping it on (therefore classified as being "ultralight"). Many are gliders and sailplanes but, when powered, these designs usually have engines smaller than 25 hp, with 10- to 15-hp being more common. Such light aircraft are not only easy and relatively fast to construct, but very fuel-efficient as well. While not suitable for regular cross-country travel, these machines provide economical sport flying at the ultimate—basic 1 to 1—level.

Aircraft in this category may be made of aluminum alloy sheet (the Windwagon); aluminum alloy tubing and fabric (the Whing Ding, Easy Riser, and Weedhopper); or wood and fabric (the Volksplane); or may have a composite construction of foam and fiber glass (brought to practical levels in the Quickie). Whereas construction time of 2000 to 5000 hours is normally required for larger aircraft powered by 100- to 250-hp engines, an ultralight design may be constructed in less than 500 hours and within as few as 150 hours if it is built from a kit having difficult formed parts completed and ready for final assembly.

Another approach frequently taken by builders anxious to get flying is to purchase a nearly completed airplane from someone who is tossing in the sponge because of a change in personal plans (e.g., moving, poor health, or lack of funds) or because another type of homebuilt has become more attractive as time goes by. Of course, the ultimate solution for many is the purchase of a completed homebuilt which may be flown at once, and then personally maintained and modified by the new owner as time permits.

In retrospect, many factors obviously overlap from one group to another, and frequently all three areas of interest interact and must be resolved before finally determining whether to build an airplane at all and, if so, which one. Do you want an airplane that cruises at 150 mph with two passengers or one that carries four, has tricycle or conventional landing gear, is all metal or steel, tube, and fabric, and may require 4000 hours of your spare time (plus $25,000) to construct? Or do you want to fly by yourself at 30 to 50 mph in a wooden or tubing and fabric ultralight that will take only 200 hours and $3500 to complete? Or maybe something in between? Because there are so many different designs to choose from at each level of complexity, a final selection becomes even more difficult to realize.

With the ever-increasing cost of new and used production aircraft, more and more people who fly or wish to fly will be forced to consider whether they want to get aloft badly enough to spend the time required to build their own airplanes. If a more sophisticated and, therefore, useful design is selected, the materials and equipment cost will of course be greater than for a simple airplane. However, this may not be as negative as it first appears because the more complex and expensive types take longer to complete. Even a $20,000 project does not loom so large if the cost is spread over a 4- to 6-year period, at a rate approximating $3000 to $4000 a year. Consider this expenditure as an investment, and assuming the project will be successfully completed and flown, the finished airplane may well be worth $45,000 to $60,000 on the current market. In fact, many custom-built or carefully restored antique aircraft sell for more than that, providing the builder with considerable profit and increase in net worth for the years of continued effort. This is another factor entering into any decision to build an airplane of your own.

It is possible to spend 4 to 6 years building an airplane, an equal amount of time flying it, and then decide that a larger (or faster, smaller, somehow different) airplane is really what you need. At this point, two choices are possible: (1) if finances permit, to complete the new homebuilt before selling the old one or (2) to sell the first one and use the proceeds to build the new, perfect airplane (perhaps with cash left over

Figure 1-2 The first Seaplane Pilots Association Brat & Corn Roast was held at Oshkosh '79. An EDO-AIR 696-3500 Amphibious Float Cessna 206 serves as a conversation piece.

for a new car, shop equipment, or whatever is needed). However, the second option limits flying to nearby fixed base rental or a friend's airplane until the latest home-built is completed.

Many builders use one of these procedures to keep an endless hobby alive and active as long as they care to fly. And being able to own different custom airplanes that can be modified and maintained as desired is not bad either. The most difficult hurdle to overcome in reaching this way of life is, quite simply, that of deciding to build and then actually completing the first airplane; unfortunately, over half the homebuilt aircraft started are never finished.

In the next chapter, we will look at the types of builders who do eventually finish a project of this magnitude—some rushing to completion in a year or two, others creeping along for 7 to 10 years. But regardless of the time span, the constant and commanding prospect of eventually flying one's own airplane, the enjoyment of a hobby demanding excellent craftsmanship, or a combination of both is necessary if a homebuilt airplane is ever to reach completion.

chapter TWO

Homebuilder Profiles

There really is no typical background or personality profile for anyone assembling a homebuilt airplane. Amateur builders from all professions, including many women as well as men, are actively joining the ranks formerly limited to hard-core mechanics, racing pilots, and custom builders.

Many sets of plans available to homebuilders contain complete instructions covering, step by step, parts fabrication and assembly procedures. In addition, most popular aircraft designs have approved sources for difficult formed and machined parts, special hardware, and welded assemblies. This means that anyone with sufficient interest and available time can build the airplane of his or her choice; prior mechanical interest or aircraft-mechanic training is not essential, although undoubtedly helpful. Regardless of your level of mechanical aptitude prior to starting your first homebuilt project, you may be sure you will have learned much and thoroughly earned a mechanic's license by the time the project is completed.

For example, tooling is needed for every part of an airplane. This means that the dimensions for each piece must be taken from the drawings and carefully laid out, full size, on either a metal template (if more than one piece is to be formed to the same part number) or on the actual material to be used in the airplane. The outline of the piece must then be rough-cut to shape on a band saw, filed to the exact outline, drilled as required, formed to shape, deburred on all edges, cadmium-plated (steel) or alodined (aluminum alloy), primed with zinc chromate or epoxy paint, and then stored with care until required for final assembly. And this is just the work required for a single part, which may be as small as a right-angle clip or as large as a wing rib or skin. When you realize that hundreds and, for larger aircraft, possibly a thousand more such items must be fabricated, the enormity of a major homebuilt aircraft program rapidly comes into focus. This is mentioned not to discourage anyone, but rather to emphasize the prime personality requirement for a successful homebuilder—and that is *perseverance* or, if you prefer, *determination*.

In a close race for second and third place on our list of homebuilder characteristics will be *self-discipline* and a *sense of organization*. If the airplane is eventually to be flown, it is necessary to set aside working time on a regular basis of so many hours per week or month. Adherence to such a program requires a great deal of self-discipline. Some progress schedule should be prepared as a guide and followed as closely as possible. Even though work may lag, the schedule should be revised to indicate how much things are falling behind and so serve as a basis for future progress. After a few months, work habits will develop into a regular pattern; the schedule can then be finalized to indicate the probable time required for completion.

A sense of organization is equally essential if the many completed pieces and hardware parts are to be found right away when needed for final assembly. Nothing is more frustrating than a fruitless search for a part you know you have completed. A log or parts list should be maintained covering every piece fabricated by group (wing, tail, and so on) and part number. To do this properly takes little time, but does require orderly preparation plus continued organization of the project as work progresses.

While each builder must provide perseverance and self-discipline, spouses, teen-aged children, or close friends can assist in the organizational department by helping to maintain records and schedules, store parts, separate hardware, and perform similar essential chores. In fact, when married, the support of your better half is most important if the various types of racket (hammering, sawing metal, and riveting), odors (primer, paint, epoxy, or polyester resin), and the general disorder, to say nothing of your withdrawal from the scene to work 10 to 20 hours per week, are to be tolerated for a period of years. Unfortunately, all of this is further compounded by the continuing drain upon available cash. Although it is not mandatory that domestic tranquility reach the level experienced by one builder I know whose wife requested a small rivet gun as a Christmas present so she could help with assembly operations, some degree of mutual enthusiasm or tolerance near that plateau will be most helpful, if not downright essential, to the completion of every homebuilt airplane.

Building an airplane should become a relaxing hobby if the experience is to be enjoyable, even though some steps are tedious and seem to take forever. However, there are no shortcuts for completion of a safe airplane, so during the building period the homebuilt becomes a great showpiece, social center, and topic of conversation. No homebuilder is ever without something to talk about and is always willing to learn a bit more about his project. This is clearly shown by watching any one of the noted designers walking about the field at Oshkosh surrounded by a cloud of his builders—like bees around a blooming flower—with each choice morsel revealed or hint dropped soaked up like a sponge and stored for future use. In short, homebuilding is an all-consuming hobby, which can also provide a great source of personal therapy for overworked business and professional people.

As a result, the movement is now entering a new growth phase, populated by fairly wealthy builders seeking a thoroughly engaging, relaxing way to spend their spare hours. This trend has induced experienced designers to enter the field with more complex but useful aircraft. Most of these models are supplemented with parts kits providing airplanes essentially similar to FAA certification standards for production aircraft performance, permitting builders who can afford the price to purchase parts and assemble an airplane in minimum time (although FAA regulations still require homebuilders to perform at least 51 percent of all construction labor). The combination of a sound airplane and reduced assembly time has natural appeal to many, and so the homebuilding hobby is simultaneously expanding in two directions, to include both the relatively wealthy as well as the less affluent.

The builders who prefer to "do it all themselves" include many who would not be able to fly any other way. They are frequently very ingenious and provide many real contributions of benefit to all homebuilders by adapting surplus parts and assemblies to successful aircraft construction. This ability extends to engines as well as flap- and landing-gear drives, windshields, and other parts. However, it is necessary to know what you are doing before taking this approach because many surplus items that supposedly have been overhauled have not been, and many parts sold "as is" are simply useless junk. So if you plan to be a minimum-cost, surplus-parts type of builder, forget it and save your money unless you know what you are buying and how the item should operate.

As a final builder profile note, it is essential that the airplane you choose suits your personal needs and intentions. This decision may involve a trade-off between time and money available for construction as well as the effect of assembly space upon airplane size. But the resulting custom airplane must suit your requirements if it is to be enjoyed when completed.

When deciding on an airplane, you should also give some thought to the type of construction preferred. Are you more comfortable with wood? Do you prefer working with sheet metal? Is steel tubing and fabric your preference? Designs using these materials are available at all levels of complexity as will be discussed in Chapter 5, but this question should be resolved as soon as the decision is made to build an airplane and before any final type is selected.

Through this approach you can narrow the field of acceptable designs down to those constructed from the preferred material. This procedure greatly simplifies the job of deciding what to build, since whichever material is selected you will have eliminated the need to consider the large number of homebuilt aircraft constructed from other materials.

I sincerely hope this chapter has focused your attention on the most basic fact that building an airplane of your own is not a simple, quick process unless you select one of the ultralight designs. While I do not wish to discourage interest in homebuilding, there is little point in leading anyone to believe that such a project can be accomplished in a short time or with little effort.

If, after rigorous self-examination, you decide that you possess the three basic homebuilder characteristics of perseverance, self-discipline, and personal organization combined with domestic support and financial capability, by all means select a design and join the growing homebuilt movement. Prepare to enjoy your airplane through many years of leisurely construction and pleasant flying as you become a member of a large, active, and enthusiastic hobby group.

Your fellow members have been drawn from all walks of life and all levels of income and mechanical ability, including accountants, airline pilots, building and construction contractors, college and school faculty members, doctors, all types of engineers, farmers, mechanics, and retired people. In fact, homebuilders include just about every profession, encompassing men and women of all ages. Some start construction without ever having built so much as a level platform for an assembly table, yet they emerge as accomplished mechanics flying their own custom airplanes. To place all this in perspective, the following chapter explores the size and scope of the homebuilt movement along with many related service organizations.

Extent
of the
Movement

Few people realize the extent of the homebuilt aircraft movement. Although no single organization keeps tabs on all of the companies and societies engaged in homebuilt activity, present sales volume is estimated by the EAA to closely approach $35 million per year worldwide. The major part of this total is expended in the United States, supporting small (and some not so small) companies selling aircraft plans and parts, assembly kits, construction tools, materials, hardware, instruments, construction manuals, flight gear, special clothing and insignia, and—not to be overlooked—memberships in specialized service organizations. These organizations include the EAA, the National Association of Sport Aircraft Designers (NASAD), the Antique Airplane Association (AAA), EAA's Antique and Classic Division, the International Aerobatic Club, the Warbirds of America, and many other smaller local and national groups.

Of the various organizations, by far the largest and most important is the EAA, which has over 60,000 members. No review of homebuilt aircraft can be undertaken without noting and praising the dedication of EAA's management and many capable volunteers who have been the driving force behind the expansion of homebuilt activity. The EAA provides a focal point for homebuilt interest, with great credit due President Paul H. Poberezny, founder of the organization, and his son, Executive Vice President Tom Poberezny, who is successfully expanding its operations.

Everyone interested in building an airplane should join the EAA, if for no other reason than to receive the association's fine magazine, *Sport Aviation*, published monthly under the able direction of Jack Cox. In addition, EAA membership provides entry into a most helpful social and working society, the local EAA chapter, where builders can swap ideas, discuss construction problems, review plans, exchange tools and parts, and find assistance with difficult details and assembly procedures. In fact, the EAA organization is based on homebuilder chapters located all over this country as well as in Canada, Europe, South America, South Africa, New Zealand, Australia, and Japan.

Chapter members welcome new builders and offer assistance based upon their own previous construction experience. Many chapters have workshops where builders may gather to socialize while cutting, forming, welding, and riveting some part or assembly of their "basement special." In the process, EAA chapter members provide backbone support for the homebuilt movement while acting as clearing centers for local activity.

When a member completes a project and all is ready for the first flight, the entire chapter usually turns out to assist with preflight preparation and witness the great event. Congratulating the builder after the ship has safely returned to earth, occasionally results in a celebration that lasts well into the next day. After all, a few years of hard spare-time effort have just been vindicated, and the relief experienced should be shared with all. Readers interested in joining the EAA will find the address listed as Reference 3.1 following this chapter.

When homebuilding started to grow by leaps and bounds a few years ago, some of the aircraft designs offered for construction were of such marginal quality and safety that the more responsible aircraft designers became extremely concerned for the future of homebuilt activity. Unfortunately, there is a great tendency for inexperienced builders to consider anything that flies as being a safe airplane—more unfortunately, this is not necessarily so.

Figure 3-1 The EAA Mini-Blimp and World War II aircraft signal the start of another super air show at Oshkosh.

Rather than have the FAA step in and place a ceiling on homebuilding by establishing prohibitively difficult inspection and licensing procedures, a group of designers formed an organization qualified to review and approve new aircraft prior to plans being offered for sale to unwary builders. And so the National Association of Sport Aircraft Designers (NASAD) came into being.

Since this organization has no formal affiliation with the EAA, NASAD approval of a design does not constitute EAA approval. (In fact, the EAA does not endorse any aircraft, although it once offered a few designs of its own.) However, designers wishing to advertise their airplanes as being approved by NASAD are encouraged to submit their plans and assembly instructions to that organization for review and classification. The procedure is usually completed within a few months, at minimum cost to the designer.

The different NASAD classifications relate more to construction complexity and whether kits are available rather than to completeness of plans or flight-handling qualities, which I consider to be equally, if not more, important. NASAD is moving toward requiring better and more fully detailed drawings as well as minimum performance criteria, but they should also include flight evaluation if the organization is to truly qualify new designs entering the homebuilt market.

At present, NASAD ratings cover three classifications based on builder experience. These are:

Class 1. Average amateur

Class 2. Experienced amateur

Class 3. Experienced experimenter

As a result, you, the builder, must determine your level of construction capability. But as a future pilot of your new airplane, don't you really want to know if it handles within your limits of flying and operational capability? Or if you desire a truly relaxing sport-flying airplane, wouldn't you like to know whether the design selected has easy handling characteristics? Learning how an airplane flies after the expenditure of thousands of dollars and years of labor does not seem the proper way to evaluate any airplane particularly if you ultimately find it does not perform or handle as expected. Nonetheless, NASAD does provide a degree of watchdog service and has made a positive contribution to homebuilt safety. Their address is listed in Reference 3.2.

Increasing numbers of builders are becoming interested in restoring antique, classic, and World War II aircraft. These older airplanes have an appeal that is mainly the result of nostalgia, but a tinge of security also enters the picture because previously flown and time-tested aircraft are obviously proven designs that have been built to established production standards. Restoring them to their former luster not only provides an appealing and crowd-pleasing airplane, but also one that has known flight characteristics. These old-timers are also probably quite safe at that, or they would have become piles of junk ages ago.

Although the FAA considers any airplane over 30 years old an antique, EAA's Antique and Classic Division requires construction prior to 1942 for antique status and between January 1, 1946 and December 31, 1950 for classic status. Not to be outdone, the Antique Airplane Association (AAA) established a "pioneer period" for aircraft manufactured between 1903 and 1914; a World War I category for planes built between 1914 and 1919; an "antique period" for aircraft flown between 1920 and 1936; and a "classic period" covering 1935 to 1941. By way of consolidating all these categories, the AAA has determined that aircraft built or awarded an Approved Type Certificate (ATC) prior to 1935 will be considered an antique airplane.

Quite understandably, everyone seems to agree that aircraft manufactured between 1942 and the end of 1945 are War Birds. Many of these planes also qualify as antiques because their original designs were approved prior to 1935. By way of example, note the fine antique Stearman War Bird in Figure 3-2, originally awarded an ATC in 1934, with a second War Bird AT-6 in the background.

The rebuilding and searching out of original parts for antique, classic, and War Bird aircraft has become a fascinating and demanding hobby for many builders. Surprisingly, although the World War II aircraft population is slowly decreasing with time more and more genuine old aircraft and replicas of antique and classic aircraft appear at Oshkosh every year. Unfortunately, restoring and maintaining these older aircraft can become an expensive pastime, and many have flight characteristics that cannot be recommended for the occasional pilot.

By way of pumping in a bit of nostalgia of our own, note the Bristol F.2 Brisfit antique replica in Figure 3-3, the authentic De Havilland Tiger Moth antique in Figure 3-4, and the antique Aircamper replica in Figure 3-5. It is easy to see how and

Figure 3-2 Shades of World War II! The trusty Stearman N2S—now an antique airplane capable of air show performance, aerobatics, crop dusting, and sport flying of any sort—but a demon when landing in severe crosswind conditions. An AT-6 is on right.

Figure 3-3 This full-scale replica of a World War I British-designed Bristol F.2 Brisfit fighter is powered by a well-concealed modern aircraft engine. Built by Vernon Ohmert, Ypsilante Township, Michigan, and shown at Oshkosh '79.

Figure 3-4 This antique and authentic variation of the De Havilland Tiger Moth is still flying.

Figure 3-5 The Aircamper is based upon one of the oldest homebuilt designs available.

why these aircraft appeal to sport-flying pilots, who can fly such craft only by building or restoring and maintaining their own. If the appeal of antique and classic aircraft has reached out with a firm grasp, References 3.3 and 3.4 will start you on your way toward ownership of an old but fascinating airplane.

Aerobatic pilots have their own specialized aircraft; support organizations; exhibitions; and local, national, and international competitions. Most of the top-rated aerobatic pilots fly aircraft designed or modified to meet their particular flight requirements or specialty maneuvers. They therefore constitute another group of homebuilders or custom-builders who prepare individualized aircraft that cannot be obtained any other way. Many pilots who are not interested in national or international competition nonetheless perform aerobatics for their own pleasure. For example, many airline pilots, locked into regimented flight procedures in their jobs but remaining free-spirited aviators at heart, find escape in personal aerobatics. As a result, they constitute a fairly large single-profession group of homebuilders, many of whom have found representation in the active organization listed in Reference 3.5.

With all these options, it is no wonder the homebuilt movement keeps growing. And to make sure serious builders can advance as fast as time and finances permit, practically all major homebuilt designs are supported by designer-originated or other approved-source kits of parts, hardware, and materials which are usually offered at reasonable cost considering the rather limited volume of orders placed at any one time. In addition, a number of supply houses offer everything from axles to windshields and wheel pants. No one needs to search very long for anything, provided he or she knows where to look (we'll cover that subject later on).

While all the foregoing basically refers to the 20,000 or so homebuilt powered aircraft and sailplanes currently flying or under construction in the United States, recent developments in ultralight aircraft tend to overwhelm established concepts of homebuilt activity (see Fig. 3-6). It is estimated that there are now over 20,000 of these very light, powered and unpowered, low-speed gliders currently in operation or under construction. Many of these aircraft are foot-launched, but the trend is toward light under-carriages and increasing amounts of power, which may soon cause ultralights to come under FAA supervision. At this writing, ultralight pilots and their aircraft are not required to be licensed. With a typical ultralight selling for around $3500, requiring fewer than 200 hours to complete and needing no licensing, it is easy to see why enthusiasm for these aircraft is growing so rapidly.

With so many different interests to satisfy, similar in purpose and intent but varying in the desired end products, it is not surprising that so many aircraft designs are available for homebuilt construction. Approximately 150 different models seem to be on the market at any one time, being offered by almost as many individual designers. Some are for wooden planes, others for all-metal, tube and fabric, or all-plastic planes. Some call for a combination of all these techniques. Some of the aircraft are easy to fly; some are not. So you can take your pick, as we shall thoroughly review in Part II, Aircraft Available.

Summing up this chapter, the homebuilt movement has expanded in 25 years from a small, select-group activity into a multimillion-dollar business involving 100,000 interested followers of the art who are currently constructing or flying approximately 30,000 light and ultralight aircraft. The builders' needs are served by a hundred or more designers and an equal or greater number of parts suppliers. If you

Figure 3-6 Australian Skycraft Scout ultralight with power plus rudder and elevator controls.

doubt this, go to Oshkosh for the EAA convention the first week of August next year and see for yourself. You may not believe it is all possible even after you've made the pilgrimage, because the displays, air shows, crowds of participants, and attending aircraft are so overwhelming; but it is real—and a genuine testimony to the current fascination with sport flying.

Let us now see how to enjoy this all-consuming hobby, which results in planes that have safety records comparable to that of certified production aircraft.

REFERENCES

3.1 Experimental Aircraft Association, Box 229, Hales Corners, WI 53130

3.2 National Association of Sport Aircraft Designers, 1756 Hanover Street, Cuyahoga Falls, OH 44221

3.3 Antique Airplane Association, P.O. Box H, Ottumwa, IA 52501

3.4 Antique and Classic Division (EAA), Box 229, Hales Corners, WI 53130

3.5 International Aerobatic Club, Inc., Box 229, Hales Corners, WI 53130

Homebuilt
Safety

Most homebuilt aircraft are constructed as direct copies or personal modifications of existing designs for which plans are available, although every year a few completely new models like that of Figure 4-1 appear as custom types designed by their builders.

Members who have been closely associated with EAA programs and progress through the years are very aware of the need to be safety-conscious during construction of each and every one of these aircraft. As a result, the organization has appointed area designees to assist, free of charge, with any member's problem that arises during the fabrication or flight test of a homebuilt airplane. In addition, design and construction forums stressing safety and the need for quality are offered during the Oshkosh convention. For serious builders, these forums are the real core and purpose of this annual gathering.

Despite all safety messages and warnings, there are still many rugged individuals who intend to learn how to fly in the airplane they are building. Some homebuilt designs are very light and small, with a minimum distance between the wing and horizontal tail surfaces. These so-called *short-coupled* aircraft can be quite sensitive

Figure 4-1   The award-winning, custom-designed and custom-built Sprinter at Oshkosh '79.

in pitch, requiring considerable pilot skill during takeoff and landing (see Ref. 4.1). To further complicate matters, many homebuilts are equipped with modified automotive engines not designed for continuous high-speed operation, providing an open invitation to powerplant failure and off-field emergency landings by relatively unskilled pilots.

Equally serious safety problems arise when builders decide to substitute more readily available materials in place of those called out on the detail construction drawings or when they modify the configuration radically without being aware of the potential danger involved. These two practices are so prevalent that most designers require every builder to sign a liability release prior to receiving a set of plans. Repeated articles in *Sport Aviation* and lectures presented at EAA meetings aim at driving home this message: *Do not alter the materials or design in any manner without first receiving written approval from the designer.*

Although no exact records are maintained by any organization, estimates of homebuilts under construction—not those flying—at any one time seem to vary from 10,000 to 15,000 aircraft. Based on personal observation, the number is more likely between 8000 to 12,000 aircraft. While this represents quite a spread, the important point is that a large number of homebuilt aircraft are under construction and flying—so the safety exposure is enormous.

Of those homebuilts completed and flying, the most successful records and most frequent usage are associated with aircraft flown by competent pilots. It is therefore impossible to overemphasize the importance of continuing to fly and remaining proficient during the entire time your airplane is being built. I'm afraid all too many homebuilders back away from a commitment to flight competency during the rather long period necessary to assemble their "dream machines," using the usual excuse of the many demands upon available time and funds. However, if the new airplane is to be enjoyed rather than destroyed, it is certainly advisable to log a minimum of 50 flight hours per year, if only at the rate of 1 hour per week around the local airport. Attempting to regain current flight status and proficiency in a strange new airplane that may have a few unexpected shakedown bugs is no way to protect those thousands of hours spent in construction. Any such philosophy is a false economy which could be injurious to both airplane and pilot.

One local EAA chapter of which I was a member included a builder completing a Thorp T-18. This two-place, tailwheel airplane is sufficiently fast and responsive to require competent pilot technique for safe operation. When the ship was about half completed we suddenly learned this builder intended to teach himself to fly in his new airplane. This would-be Wright or Curtiss pioneer had never piloted an airplane but was sure the procedure was quite simple, particularly if some of his fellow builders were licensed pilots. We virtually carried this character out to the local airstrip and promptly deposited him in a J-3 Cub to receive flight instruction in a tailwheel-type airplane. He is gradually acquiring a private pilot rating and should have 150 hours or so when his T-18 is finished.

Of course, 150 hours does not provide sufficient experience for checking any airplane on its first flight, again a safety consideration that is frequently overlooked in the rush of enthusiasm to finally "get 'er flying." Unfortunately, one of the major causes of homebuilt fatalities is the urge to surge aloft, which often results in overlooking the need for detail inspection, powerplant ground testing, and trial hops along the runway *prior* to any first flight. And when owners cannot wait for an experienced pilot to schedule time for the initial shakedown flights, it is not unusual to find them eagerly substituting their own skills. However, these may be inadequate if powerplant or stability problems develop, frequently followed by a major or fatal accident.

As a parallel thought, if your flying time is rather limited or your technique a bit rusty, construction of a two-place or larger airplane should be seriously considered. That second seat will permit an experienced pilot to get you thoroughly familiar with your new airplane—a safety consideration of prime importance.

If the basic rules of homebuilt safety were carefully followed, the annual accident rate for homebuilts would be lower than that for FAA certified production aircraft. As it is, the percentage of homebuilt accidents closely parallels that for all general aviation aircraft. (The *"general aviation"* fleet includes all active aircraft with the exception of commercial airline and military planes. It includes both fixed- and rotary-wing, powered and unpowered configurations.)

To the extent possible, the EAA maintains files on all homebuilt accidents, with particular emphasis on aerobatic mishaps, whether they involve experimental aircraft (homebuilt or modified production types) or the more numerous certified aerobatic models. The latest data available indicates that homebuilt aircraft are involved in a small percentage of all reported accidents—even in the aerobatic category, which contains a greater percentage of homebuilt aircraft than does the personal aircraft category (used for business or pleasure flying). *Design for Safety*, listed in Reference 4.2, includes a more thorough discussion of this subject.

Of the approximately 200,000 single-engine piston planes licensed and flying in the United States at this time, about 8000, or 4 percent, are homebuilts. As a result of the EAA and associated volunteer safety effort, all homebuilt airplanes are involved in less than 4.5 percent of all small aircraft general aviation accidents. This is similar to the percentage ratio of registered homebuilt aircraft noted above, representing an operational record approaching that of certified production aircraft. And that's a record in which the EAA membership takes justifiable pride while working steadily to lower the totals year after year.

It seems quite possible that the homebuilt accident rate would even better that of certified production aircraft if every homebuilder would follow these rules:

1. Attend design and flight forums at Oshkosh.

2. Never alter plans or substitute materials without first receiving written permission from the designer.

3. Remain proficient by flying at least 50 hours per year while completing the new airplane.

4. Thoroughly ground-check all systems, particularly fuel delivery, and test-hop a new or modified airplane a few times prior to the first flight.

5. Never attempt a first flight of a new or modified airplane without having 5000 or more total pilot hours and current proficiency.

6. Receive thorough and competent flight instruction in the new airplane before flying solo (unless the builder is a very experienced pilot).

This code is not difficult to follow and is really a matter of common sense, yet all items are equally important and many are frequently ignored. Since practically all homebuilt accidents arise from overlooking one of these recommendations, they should be carefully followed, even if Item 6 means construction of a two-place machine instead of that sleek single-place. It is essential to *think safety*; flying an airplane is not like driving an automobile and requires a conservative approach if experience is to be acquired.

The fact that homebuilt aircraft can equal or better the safety record of production aircraft is quite remarkable and represents a positive tribute to the capabilities of the many designers of these small aircraft. There are over 100 different homebuilt models to chose from, and we shall review most of the designers and their aircraft in the next section. This material includes specifications, photos, brief descriptions, and three-view drawings of most of the aircraft currently available for home construction.

REFERENCES

4.1 John W. Olcott, "Bede Turns It Loose," *Flying,* October 1974.

4.2 David B. Thurston, *Design for Safety*, McGraw-Hill, New York, 1980, pp. 14–17.

Aircraft
Available

Designs
and
Designers

Although there are more homebuilt designs than designers, there are plenty of both. Depending upon the field of interest of the individual designers, their aircraft vary from extremely simple but rather fragile construction through the entire range of monoplanes, biplanes, and canards. They include some of composite construction, some of tube and fabric, and a few all-metal types designed essentially in accordance with FAA's Federal Air Regulations (FAR) Part 23 certification specifications.

You may select a sailplane (either a high-performance, unpowered or powered model, or a training type); an aerobatic monoplane or biplane; a small, high-performance aircraft requiring considerable piloting skill and surfaced runways; a purely sport-flying, open- or closed-cockpit monoplane or biplane that is easily handled from small fields; a cross-country, four-place aircraft; a large or small amphibian; an extremely efficient, one- or two-place canard model; a World War I or II military replica; a copy of an antique or classic design, and so on and on. The list of options is almost endless, occasionally defying proper classification, particularly when considering the difficulty or complexity of construction.

The spectrum of building materials and types of assembly covers virtually anything you might want for any kind of airplane you might decide to build. For example, a two-place cabin biplane can be built from riveted aluminum-alloy sheet metal and extrusions, from welded chrome-moly tubing plus wood and fabric, or from a combination of these materials. Possibly you prefer a two-place monoplane assembled from steel tube and fabric, or riveted aluminum alloy and extrusions, or composite (foam and fiber glass) construction, or a mixture of these materials. They are all available for your selection.

DEFINING YOUR DESIGN REQUIREMENTS

For the beginning homebuilder, one of life's more critical problems arises with the need to select an airplane design. Since the final decision will be around for a number of years, it is preferable to have the airplane chosen develop into a pleasing rather than a plaguing project. In reaching this determination consideration should be given to the following criteria with regard to your specific requirements:

1. Space available for construction

2. Airplane configuration and desired characteristics

3. Preferred seating capacity

4. Type of construction best suited to your workshop experience and equipment, if any

5. Fabricated parts or kits available

6. Probable cost of the engine and propeller specified

7. Types of airports likely to be used

8. Handling qualities compatible with your flight experience

All these items are equally important regardless of their order of presentation and break down any final decision into three basic components. The first three items relate to *airplane size*. Items 4 through 6 help determine the *type of construction, material, overall time*, and *cost* required to complete assembly. The last two items define essential *flight characteristics* needed to satisfy your particular requirements. Expanding these items in the order presented should further assist in completing that critical decision; probably leading to one or more designs suitable for your use at least until the airplane has been flown for a few years.

Space Available

Experience has shown this to be an increasingly important consideration as a project moves along toward completion. While we will discuss working space at length in Chapter 9, remember that at some point every homebuilt must have the various structural components assembled, and the larger the airplane, the larger the basement, shed, garage, hangar, or outside assembly area must be.

If a big airplane is selected, suitable shop space may have to be constructed, but this will add considerable cost and time to the homebuilding program. While assembly space should not adversely affect your decision regarding airplane size, it is advisable to plan for suitable facilities at the time a design is selected and so include related costs accordingly. The alternative is a sudden realization that more space is necessary when well into construction—costing additional time as well as money not previously scheduled and possibly not available when needed.

Airplane Configuration and Desired Characteristics

I suppose just about every pilot would like to own an airplane which cruises at 200 mph and lands at 35 mph; is able to perform aerobatics with ease thanks to its perfectly coordinated controls which are responsive right into the stall; is capable of carrying four passengers plus baggage for 800 or more miles cross-country; is readily convertible from an open cockpit to an enclosed cabin; costs under $5000 to construct; and can be assembled in less than 1000 hours. Of course, such an "ideal" vehicle does not exist at the present state-of-the-art of small aircraft design and fabrication. But homebuilt models capable of satisfying one or more of these criteria are available for your consideration.

Do you want a sleek, efficient monoplane or biplane which requires considerable pilot skill and hard-surfaced runways? Can you handle such a plane with ease and relaxed enjoyment? Is aerobatics your specialty? This would narrow your choice down considerably to those proven successful aerobatic biplanes or monoplanes performing at air shows and major competitions. Did you start flying back in the 1930s, and would you like to restore or build a replica of one of the so-called classic or antique aircraft? The swing back to nostalgia in fashion and music is spilling over into these older machines, with many different types taking to the air in increasing numbers every year.

If your interest parallels that of the great majority of homebuilders, you will select plans for an airplane that is relaxing and pleasant to fly, seats two to four people, has a rugged and relatively maintenance-free construction with established sources for difficult formed parts and sub-assemblies, can be readily serviced by the builder, does not guzzle alarming quantities of gas, and can be operated from a 2000- to 3000-foot runway. While cruising speed may be important to you, it is secondary to pleasant handling characteristics and the pure enjoyment of flying. In other words, an airplane that provides full satisfaction from this supreme hobby of sport flying.

I doubt that any single homebuilt design will ever satisfy every pilot-builder, but I do know such a variety of designs exists that any serious builder should be able to find the "perfect airplane" for almost any particular set of requirements, including amphibious operation. At any rate, defining your preference for basic airplane characteristics, configuration, style, and cosmetic appeal should considerably narrow the field of candidates—similar to entering the final round of any beauty contest.

Preferred Seating Capacity

Do you just want to "get away from it all" and float around up there by yourself? If so, will you want to do only that 3 to 5 years from now when the airplane is finally flying? And for a few years after that great moment? Or will you then want to share flying with your friends, spouse, and children?

If you wish to learn aerobatics in your new machine, things would progress much faster and more safely if a second seat were included for a qualified flight instructor. If you already have aerobatic proficiency, possibly a single-place plane will do—but how about occasionally taking a friend aloft or the possibility of making cross-country flights with some frequency by way of enjoying the utility built into all aircraft? So do you really want just a single-place airplane, or would two seats plus some range be more useful and therefore desirable?

If you are a conservative pilot, will you want to use your plane for business and pleasure trips? This might require four seats plus room for baggage and adequate fuel capacity for a 4- to 5-hour trip. Or will two seats and less range be satisfactory? It would certainly be easier to build. If the need for four seats is infrequent, seating for two plus baggage space which can also be used for two jump seats would seem an acceptable compromise. If fuel capacity is adequate for the range desired, the resulting airplane will be lighter, less costly, and require less building time than would a full four-place airplane.

Of course, builders who intend to learn to fly in their new homebuilt should never consider a design with less than two seats. Teaching yourself to fly in a single-seater is both illegal and an open invitation to suicide, so all beginning builders should seriously consider starting with at least a two-place configuration.

Type of Construction

While familiarity with working metal or wood or using associated cutting and forming tools is helpful, such experience is not essential for successful completion of a homebuilt airplane. Many people who, quite literally, have never nailed or joined anything together have succeeded in doing a creditable job of construction by reading the available building manuals and carefully following the airplane's detail design drawings. Having a friend who has built an airplane or who is an aircraft and power-plant (A&P) mechanic is a great help, as is proximity or access to an active EAA chapter.

If you have no prior experience with or any preference for a particular construction medium, which one should you select, and why? Wood is probably a bit easier to work with—and the tools required are both readily available and somewhat simpler to use than those required for metal—but sawdust does have a way of getting all over everything. And, while some may disagree, the life of a wooden airplane will be shorter than that of an all-metal or tube and fabric assembly unless the plane is kept hangared. Moisture and the accompanying dry rot are the nemesis of wooden airplanes, regardless of the finish used. Frequent and thorough maintenance inspection of the highly stressed areas is therefore required to assure structural integrity. While this may not be a great chore, such inspections are more critical for wooden than for metal aircraft.

If you select a steel-tube fuselage structure, possibly with all-metal wings or wood spars and metal ribs plus fabric covering, someone must be able to weld the assembly to aircraft standards. If you cannot do this yourself, do you know someone who can? Or can a welded fuselage assembly be purchased for the design selected?

Regardless of the major construction material selected, most aircraft will require some welding, such as the engine-mount or control-stick assembly, so the availability of welding assistance or the need to develop welding capability is something that every homebuilder should seriously consider.

All-metal construction (almost certainly of aluminum alloy sheet and extruded sections) lends itself to the most precise structural analysis, assuring adequate flight strength provided the drawings are followed in detail. Although sheet metal normally requires more tooling and building time than does wood, ample repayment is realized from increased service life and reduced maintenance.

For most available designs, whether wood or metal, some edge may be taken off the prospect of never-ending labor by purchasing formed or prefabricated parts from approved supply sources. The designers frequently designate acceptable manufacturers for various components of their aircraft and maintain follow-up surveillance to assure continued quality.

Since aircraft of all types are offered in all materials, determining which construction medium you prefer will narrow the selection process considerably. You may decide to assemble your "dream airplane" from wood, composite plastic, steel tube and fabric (perhaps with wooden spars), all metal, or, possibly, a combination of all these materials. In the final analysis, the type of construction selected should depend upon the material with which you will be most comfortable.

Fabricated Parts or Kits Available

If you have decided to build an airplane in order to become familiar with its construction and maintenance and are willing and able to trade dollars for time, the availability of high-quality fabricated parts and difficult assemblies will be a most important consideration in your design selection. Even builders who prefer to make every part themselves will usually find that it is better to purchase some weld assemblies or machined pieces from sources having proper tooling. Building assembly fixtures for a critical part or assembly can frequently take so long that it is just impractical to construct such tooling for one airplane. In this case, the item should be purchased rather than built.

This make-or-buy decision can influence the choice of design whenever it is desirable to get flying as quickly as possible. Even with all parts purchased, a year or so will probably be required to complete assembly, but the time span could have been 5 years or more if all parts had to be tooled and built from scratch.

As an added note, the price of purchased parts will serve to indicate or determine the price of your completed airplane (at least as far as the airframe is concerned). When a complete parts kit is available, purchase of the engine and propeller not only immediately determines the final airplane cost (except for equipment and finishing), but also permits construction as a pleasant and fairly rapid assembly program rather than a tooling, fabrication, and assembly process that may take many years.

All of which indicates that the availability of kits and parts can be an important consideration in the selection of any homebuilt airplane design.

Engine and Propeller—Probable Cost

The type of engine selected for any homebuilt design represents a large percentage of the completed airplane cost. Since we will discuss powerplant requirements and operation at some length in Chapter 8, it is sufficient to note here that any design considered should have installation drawings for a powerplant acceptable to you. The details should include an engine mount designed for a specific-model engine. It is not enough to specify a Lycoming 0-320, Continental C90, or whatever; the exact engine designation, such as 0-320-B3B, for example, should be included. Engines have many accessory and magneto variations that can develop installation clearance problems unless the mount is designed to accept a specific model.

You may be considering using a modified automobile engine as a matter of basic economy. Before making any final decision, remember that automotive engines are not only heavy but are not designed for the sustained high-power output required for aircraft operation. The typical car moves along on 30 to 40 percent or less of rated power; aircraft normally cruise at 60 to 70 percent power. This means that automobile engine bearings, rods, pistons, valves, pumps, and so on are built for a different set of conditions. Although conversions are available to increase the life of automotive engines, most of them do not provide the safety of dual ignition, even though their price may actually exceed that of a good remanufactured or fully overhauled certified aircraft engine.

Again we find a criteria that can best be satisfied by what you prefer, can afford, and will be most comfortable with. My personal preference is for the 4-cylinder, 90-hp Continental C-90-16F, the 100-hp Continental 0-200-A, the 108- to 125-hp Lycoming 0-235-G2B, the 160-hp Lycoming 0-320-B3B, and the 180-hp Lycoming 0-360-A1F6D. I also like the 6-cylinder, 145-hp Continental 0-300D, the 210-hp Continental models 10-360-A through G, and the 250-hp Lycoming 0-540-A4B5 or -A4D5.

As a bonus, many of these engines may be equipped with constant-speed propellers for superior performance, but if your interest is primarily sport flying for leisurely relaxation, a constant-speed propeller is not necessary and probably not desirable because it will weigh more, cost more, and require more maintenance than will a fixed-pitch type. But when you are looking for short-field takeoff, maximum climb, and aerobatic performance, the constant-speed propeller comes into its own.

At present (1980), remanufactured or completely overhauled certified aircraft engines range in price from about $3500 for the smaller models to $10,000 for a 6-cylinder model in top shape. Of course, turbosupercharged versions cost about $2000 to $3000 more for the 180- to 250-hp engines.

Fixed-pitch propellers are available in wood or metal (with metal types delivering about 10 percent more efficiency) and will cost from $150 to $250 for moderate power ratings. Modern, constant-speed propellers have metal blades, weigh about twice as much as fixed-pitch propellers capable of handling similar power, and cost about five times as much. As usual, performance "costs," but don't buy more than you require; which brings up our last two items covering desired flight characteristics.

Types of Airports

Presumably most of your flying will be from a local airport, or will you frequently be flying cross-country in your new homebuilt? The answer to this question relates to the type of takeoff and landing characteristics required from your airplane. Will you normally be flying from hard-surfaced, dirt, gravel, or grass runways? Certainly if home base will be a dirt or gravel strip, you do not want a plane with small wheels or one requiring a long ground run. You need short takeoff and landing (STOL) performance. Conversely, if a high-speed design approaching at 80 mph or more is selected, your base airport must have a hard-surfaced runway at least 3000 feet long, and even longer for more sophisticated aircraft capable of high-speed, cross-country, and instrument flight rules (IFR) operation. In fact, if IFR equipment is to be installed, your home airport should, ideally, have one or more approved types of instrument landing systems (ILS) to fully utilize your airplane's capability in poor weather.

Many small airports are located so that steep climb-outs and equally steep approaches are mandatory for safe operation. To provide the STOL performance required, any design selected must have adequate power and a relatively low wing loading (preferably less than 12 lb/sq ft of wing area—as determined by dividing airplane gross weight by the wing area). If the airplane is not of high drag configuration, as is a biplane with all its wing brace wires or an amphibian with a bulky hull, flaps or spoilers will be required for steep descent and to keep the plane from floating down the runway when flaring from an approach that was a bit too fast.

Climb-out is improved by a constant-speed propeller as well as by a low power loading. As shown in Figure 5-1, the lower the combination of wing and power loading (W_T) the better the climb performance; for STOL operation, W_T should be no more than 27 and preferably nearer 24 (the 65-hp J-3 Cub has a W_T of 25.6 and excellent STOL performance, although the wing loading at 6.83 lb/sq ft is a bit light for bumpy air). If possible, balanced conditions, with both wing and power loadings near 12, will provide a good compromise. This requires about 115 hp for an airplane with a gross weight of 1400 lb. If you can provide 125 to 150 hp for the same weight and wing loading, climb performance will improve accordingly (although OPEC members, unfortunately, will delight in the added fuel consumption).

Possibly you are interested in flying to your lakeside camp. If so, is an amphibian necessary, or can you make the trip from water to water at either end? In that case a seaplane rather than an amphibian may be your answer. However, if you wish to fly in during the winter by landing on an ice- or snow-covered lake, landing gear is essential for installation of snow skis.

The various designs you consider, and certainly your final choice, must satisfy conditions at your local airport, and your particular operational needs. If a compromise becomes necessary, local airport conditions should be favored because that is where most of your flying will take place in the years ahead. So choose an airplane capable of satisfying local as well as personal requirements.

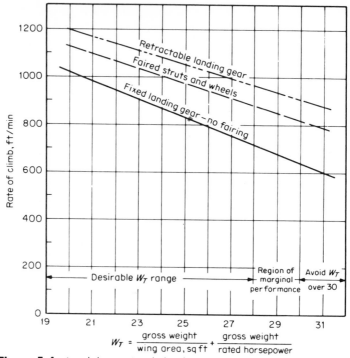

Figure 5-1 Landplane (tricycle landing gear) climb rate versus landing gear fairing and W_T.

Handling Qualities and Flight Experience

Note that the heading is not "handling qualities desired." Probably all of us would like to fly an airplane of greater performance or more demanding characteristics than we can safely handle under adverse conditions; although we should more properly consider what we can take care of while feeling relaxed and enjoying the scenery. After all, isn't that what sport flying is all about? This is a decision requiring you to wrestle with an honest analysis of how much flying is done every year, as well as your actual level of current flight proficiency and familiarity with the latest flight regulations. Really, just how proficient are you now and will you be when your homebuilt is completed? Don't build more than you can handle unless it has two or more seats permitting you to take flight instruction prior to solo operation.

This is one important determination only *you* can make; don't let your friends convince you to build an airplane beyond your flight capability, because you will never enjoy your airplane if you do.

As for me, I'll opt for a faired tricycle fixed-gear, all-metal, 180-hp, four-place design that handles with ease. I would also throw in at least a 3500-foot-long, hard-surfaced runway for good measure, along with instrument approach systems, an angle of attack (AOA) indicator, and a heated pitot. Then I'll feel comfortable. What

TABLE 5-1   Aircraft Attending EAA Convention—Seventh-Day Statistics

	1977	1978	1979
Custom-Built	458	448	381
Antique	181	193	183
Classic	530	595	549
Rotorcraft	33	32	28
Warbird	153	144	124
Replica	6	5	11
Special	11	16	19
Ultralight	—	24	66
Static display	4	1	16
Total	1376	1458	1377

do you really require? Whatever it is, that is what you should build, and the above review should materially help you make that decision. While there are many different items and criteria to be considered, there are also many designs to choose from.

Table 5-1 is an indication of the diversity of designs available to homebuilders. It is a compilation of the different classifications of aircraft posted after the seventh day of the 1979 EAA annual convention at Oshkosh. The list certainly contains something for everyone, running from one-of-a-kind, custom-built aircraft to restored Golden Oldies, World War II aircraft, and a growing number of ultralight designs.

DESIGNERS

The designer's reputation and cooperation are considerations in selecting a design, particularly for those builders searching out their first airplane. The fact that a design may have been around for some time is not as critical as builders' opinions of how complete and accurate the plans proved to be during construction, further supported by pilot comments regarding flight characteristics of the resulting aircraft.

These are two completely different subjects. The plans may be "dogs" to follow, requiring much guesswork and builder input or imagination, yet the completed airplane may fly beautifully and look quite handsome as well. Or the plans may be complete and easy to follow, only to find the resulting airplane is a real handful in flight.

This conflict need not be difficult to resolve. Talk to people who have built and flown the various models you are considering for final selection and decide accordingly. By attending EAA chapter meetings and local fly-ins over a six month period, plus the annual convention at Oshkosh, you should be able to canvass many builders and inspect the various completed aircraft as well. Take time to decide because you will have to live with the resulting choice for many years.

In the initial literature describing their aircraft, many designers will advise whether the individual airplane is difficult to build or fly. As an example, the Sequoia 300 brochure clearly states that plans will not normally be sold to anyone with less than 500 hours flying time and much of that time must have been in high-performance, retractable-gear aircraft. In fact, military and airline pilot experience plus an A&P license is the preferred background for anyone considering building this exceptionally fast plane.

One great fear of all designers is the possibility of developing a series of "pen pals" who write about every facet of the plans purchased and each construction problem that develops over the years. This can become so burdensome that a designer may turn away from correspondence, with the result that serious questions from responsible builders remain unanswered. To avoid this discouraging possibility, choose a design that has either an established construction manual, a regular builder's letter, a class association for dissemination of problems and solutions as well as notices of class activity, or, ideally, all three forms of communication.

If your "perfect" airplane requires some modification of a basic design, be sure the designer will approve your alterations before building that model. Many designers do not take kindly to tampering with their aircraft. Also, some proposed changes may result in undesirable or dangerous flight characteristics. Since you will be associated with the airplane under construction for some time and may need advice from time to time during assembly, I recommend that you get to know, or at least contact, the designer to establish a working relationship before purchasing your plans. If this is not possible, you should choose another airplane and a different designer.

During this phase of selection, bear in mind that no designer is going to be overjoyed if suggested configuration or materials modifications will result in an unsafe airplane. After all, you will be jeopardizing the designer's reputation through any such arbitrary action, to say nothing of tampering with his brainchild. In that regard, it is most important to realize that no set of plans or designer's reputation can prevent trouble if you make improper alterations in the basic design or substitutions of parts or materials during construction.

For the above reasons, if you are to enjoy your project, the final decision regarding homebuilt plans should be balanced between the designer and the desired airplane configuration.

The following two chapters contain data for 105 different aircraft. This should cover the field in sufficient depth to satisfy any individual set of specifications. I'm sure many of these designs will meet your requirements, thereby pleasantly complicating the process of final selection.

Builder's Choice — Airplanes Galore

In writing this chapter, I was presented with a great challenge when it became necessary to classify the various designs according to some system that would permit reasonably ready reference. Should they be classified according to seating capacity, cruising speed, number of wings, conventional or unconventional configuration, materials of construction, difficulty of construction, hours of work required, completion cost, difficulty of operation, some combination of these factors, or what?

Since the following aircraft are all considered to be reasonably safe if flown by a pilot with some degree of proficiency, the "difficulty of operation" rating can be eliminated without further consideration. Finally, and after some juggling, I decided that classifying the different designs alphabetically by category—landplanes, helicopters, sailplanes and gliders, seaplanes, and ultralights—would be according to types of builder interest, and so that is the system used. Antiques, pioneer and classic aircraft, replicas, and one-of-a-kind custom designs are gathered together as a separate group and discussed in Chapter 7.

The three-view drawings, dimensional data, and performance values for these aircraft represent the latest information obtained directly from the various designers. As such, the material should be correct, but I cannot personally guarantee the accuracy of all items. When available, a thumbnail sketch of the designer's background qualifications as well as a photo of the designer have been included with the descriptions of the aircraft. In addition, the prices of plans and kits have been noted when available; however, these may be subject to some increases with time.

The airframe construction materials called for are also listed for each homebuilt so you can run through the different designs and select the type of construction preferred. This approach will rapidly reduce the overwhelming field to a few choice aircraft that incorporate the construction, configuration, seating, and performance desired. (The *airframe* is the basic structure of the airplane, including the wings, tail surfaces, fuselage or hull, cowling, engine mount, control system, and landing gear. Or, more simply, the load-carrying structure of the airplane.)

For readers wishing to find a specific model, the index includes a cross-reference listing of all these aircraft under the heading "Aircraft designs" as well as under the designer's or manufacturer's name. As a reminder for anyone wishing to write to any of these companies or designers for additional information, please enclose a self-addressed, stamped envelope.

With this brief introduction, let us review the 105 different homebuilts which constitute the real heart of this book.

LANDPLANES

It is quite apparent that land operation is more popular than water, since we have 71 powered designs in this category in addition to all the helicopters, gliders, and sailplanes that operate from land. The variety of construction materials, airplane configurations, and seating arrangements included should satisfy anyone's requirements while offering some depth of selection. For want of a better method, the various manufacturers or designers have been listed in alphabetical order rather than by airplane name or model.

Ace Aircraft Mfg. Co.
106 Arthur Road
Asheville, NC 28806

Designation: Model D Baby Ace
Seating: Single place
Type: High-wing monoplane
Aerobatic: No
Construction Material: Steel tubing, wood, fabric
Information Kit: $5
Plans Cost: $50
Kits Available: For materials from manufacturer

Span: 26 ft 5 in
Length: 17 ft 8.75 in
Height: 6 ft 7.75 in
Wing Area: 112.3 ft^2
Power: 65 to 85 hp
Empty Weight: 575 lb
Useful Load: 375 lb
Gross Weight: 950 lb
Stalling Speed: 40 mph
Cruising Speed: 90 mph

Designation: Model E Junior Ace
Seating: Two side by side
Type: High-wing monoplane
Aerobatic: No
Construction Material: Steel tubing, wood, fabric
Information Kit: $5
Plans Cost: $65
Kits Available: For materials and some weld assemblies

Span: 26 ft 5 in
Length: 17 ft 8.75 in
Height: 6 ft 7.75 in
Wing Area: 112.3 ft^2
Power: 65 to 85 hp
Empty Weight: 575 lb
Useful Load: 375 lb
Gross Weight: 950 lb
Stalling Speed: 45 mph
Cruising Speed: 90 mph

Photo courtesy of Ace Aircraft Manufacturing Company.

Thurman G. Baird

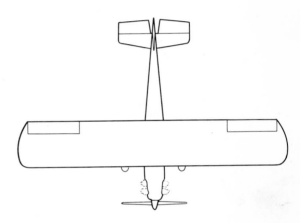

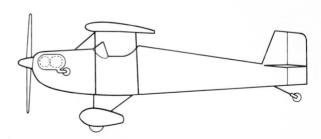

Ace A/C (cont'd.)

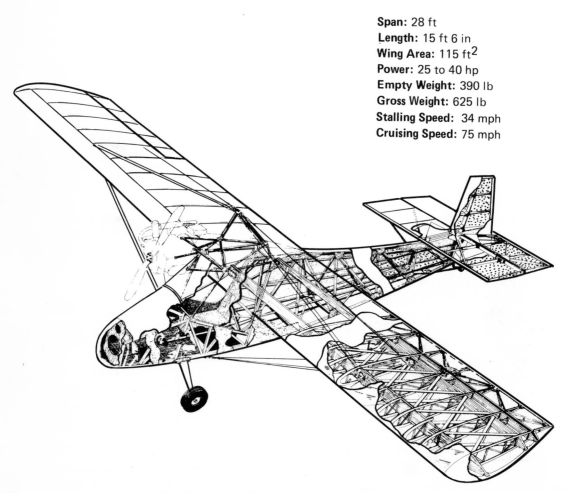

Designation: Flaglor Scooter
Seating: Single place
Type: High-wing monoplane
Aerobatic: No
Construction Material: Steel tubing, wood, fabric
Information Kit: $5
Plans Cost: $35
Kits Available: For parts, materials, and weld assembly

Span: 28 ft
Length: 15 ft 6 in
Wing Area: 115 ft^2
Power: 25 to 40 hp
Empty Weight: 390 lb
Gross Weight: 625 lb
Stalling Speed: 34 mph
Cruising Speed: 75 mph

Acro Sport, Inc.
P. O. Box 462
Hales Corners, WI 53130

The Pober Pixie, Acro Sport, and Acro II were designed by Paul Poberezny, founder and president of the Experimental Aircraft Association and well known to all active homebuilders. These three aircraft represent proven designs based on the Heath Parasol and Pitts aerobatic biplane configurations.

Designation: Pober Pixie
Seating: Single place
Type: High-wing monoplane
Aerobatic: No
Construction Material: Steel Tubing, wood, fabric
Information Kit: $4
Plans Cost: $45
Kits Available: For materials and weld assemblies from Wag-Aero, Box 181, Lyons, WI 53148

Span: 29 ft 10 in
Length: 17 ft 3 in
Wing Area: 134.25 ft^2
Power: 40 to 65 hp
Empty Weight: 543 lb
Gross Weight: 900 lb
Stalling Speed: 30 mph
Cruising Speed: 83 mph

Photo courtesy of Acro Sport, Inc.

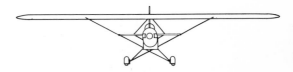

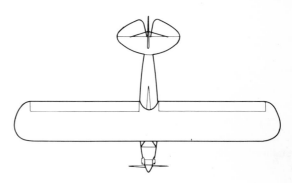

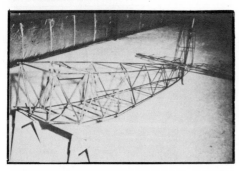

The Pober Pixie fuselage prior to adding on the wing cabane struts, landing gear fittings, and other smaller fittings.

Acro Sport, Inc (cont'd)

Designation: Acro Sport and Super Acro
Seating: Single place
Type: Biplane
Aerobatic: Unlimited
Construction Material: Steel tubing, wood, fabric
Information Kit: $4
Plans Cost: $60 for Acro Sport; $15 for Super Acro wing
Kits Available: From Wag-Aero

Photo courtesy of Acro Sport, Inc.

Note: Acro Sport II is also available as a two-seat version of Acro Sport

Span: Upper: 19 ft 7 in, lower: 19 ft 1 in
Length: 17 ft 6 in
Height: 6 ft
Wing Area: 116 ft^2
Power: 100 to 200 hp
Empty Weight: 844 lb
Gross Weight: 1350 lb
Stalling Speed: 50 mph
Cruising Speed: 130 mph

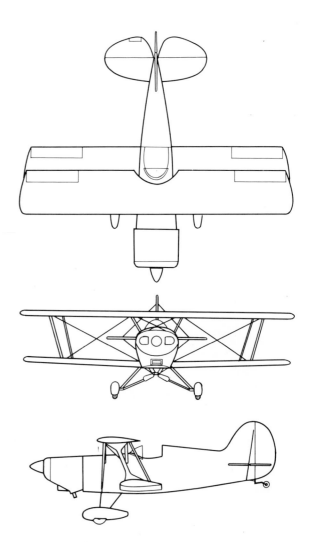

The strength and light weight of steel tubing, combined with careful design and construction, produce a fuselage that is exceptionally strong.

Aerosport, Incorporated
Box 278
Holly Springs, NC 27540

The late Harris L. Woods, E. B. Trent, and
R. D. Fehlner have designed a safe, sturdy,
and simple airplane. Over 50 years of
aeronautical design, engineering, and
fabrication experience has been incorporated
into the Scamp-A. Each part has been fully
stress-analyzed to give the structure 6 "G"
capability. The Scamp's unique "T-tail"
configuration is designed and incorporated
into the structure to provide better stall
and spin control. Controllability and light
control forces are a design criteria.

Photo courtesy of Aerosport, Incorporated.

Designation: Scamp
Seating: Single place
Type: Biplane
Aerobatic: Limited
Construction Material: All metal
Information Kit: $5
Plans Cost: $50 with construction manual
Kits Available: From Aerosport

Span: 17.5 ft
Length: 16.7 ft
Wing Area: 102.5 ft^2
Power: VW 1700 to 1834 cc
Empty Weight: 530 lb
Gross Weight: 768 lb
Stalling Speed: 42 mph
Cruising Speed: 90 mph

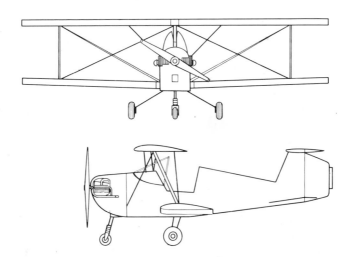

Aircraft Specialties Co.
Box 1074
Saugus, CA 91350

R. W. (Bob) Hovey started his aviation career designing, building, and flying model aircraft. Following his aero-engineering education, Bob joined Lockheed in 1943 and has contributed to the design of aircraft ranging from the P-38 to the Lunar Orbiter Spacecraft Program and rotary wing composite aircraft. His Wing Ding II and Beta Bird designs are simply constructed aircraft.

Photo courtesy of Aircraft Specialties Co.

R. W. (Bob) Hovey

Designation: Wing Ding II
Seating: Single place
Type: Biplane
Aerobatic: No
Construction Material: Tubing, wood, fabric
Information Kit: $2
Plans Cost: $20 with construction description
Kits Available: Materials sources listed

Span: 16.3 ft
Wing Area: 98 ft^2
Power: 12 to 15 hp
Empty Weight: 122 lb
Useful Load: 188 lb
Gross Weight: 310 lb
Stalling Speed: 26 mph
Cruising Speed: 45 mph

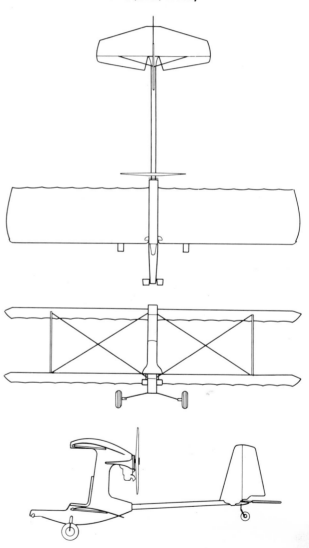

Aircraft Specialties Co. (cont'd)

Designation: Beta Bird
Seating: Single place
Type: High-wing monoplane
Aerobatic: No
Construction Material: Tubing, wood, sheet
　　metal, fabric
Information Kit: $5
Plans Cost: $60 with instruction book
Kits Available: Complete kit from company

Photo courtesy of Aircraft Specialties Co.

Span: 25 ft 6 in
Power: VW 1200 to 1600 cc
Empty Weight: 405 lb
Gross Weight: 630 lb

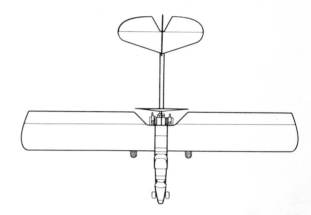

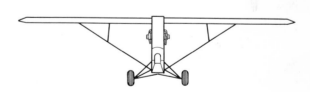

Björn (Andy) Andreasson
Collins Väg 22B
23012 Höllviksnäs, Sweden

Andy Andreasson

Photo courtesy of Björn Andreasson.

Photo courtesy of Björn Andreasson

A well-known aircraft design engineer with over 40 years experience in Sweden, Denmark, and America (Convair), Andy Andreasson is currently a member of the Saab design team. An active pilot, his work reflects the background gained from a range of aircraft designs encompassing trainers, aerobatic aircraft, and turbine transports as well as his basic interest in homebuilt aircraft.

Designation: BA-4B
Seating: Single place
Type: Biplane
Aerobatic: Unlimited (per FAR-23, APP.A, category A)
Construction Material: All metal
Information Kit: $5
Plans Cost: $100 with 60 drawings, instructions, material list
Kits Available: Not at present time

Span: 17.7 ft
Length: 15.3 ft
Height: 5.8 ft
Wing Area: 90 ft^2
Power: 65 to 130 hp
Empty Weight: 570 lb
Gross Weight: 880 lb aerobatic, 990 lb utility
Stalling Speed: 50 mph
Cruising Speed: 135 mph

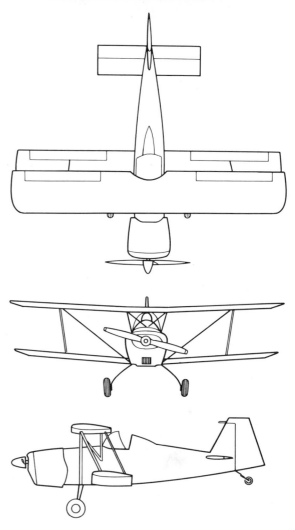

Note: The BA-6, a single-seat monoplane of wood and fabric, is also available.

48

B. Andreasson (cont'd)

Photo courtesy of Saab Scania.

Designation: BA-11
Seating: Two in tandem
Type: Biplane
Aerobatic: Unlimited
Construction Material: All metal
Information Kit: $5
Plans Cost: $200
Kits Available: Not at this time

Span: Upper wing: 19.4 ft
Length: 19 ft
Wing Area: 118 ft^2
Power: Lyc. AEIO-360 of 200 hp
Gross Weight: 1550 lb
Stalling Speed: 45 mph
Cruising Speed: 155 mph

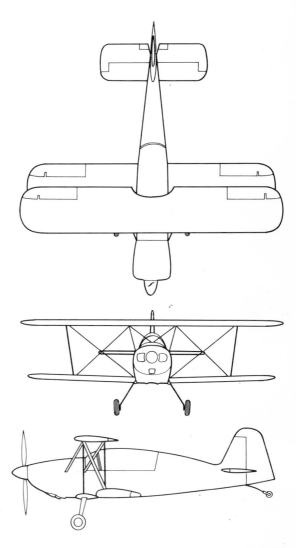

B. Andreasson (cont'd)

Designation: MFI-9B (FAA certified design)
Seating: Two side by side
Type: Shoulder-wing monoplane
Aerobatic: Limited
Construction Material: All metal
Information Kit: $5
Plans Cost: $200 with material and equipment
      lists, and flight and operation manuals
Kits Available: Not at this time

Photo courtesy of Olle Sjöberg.

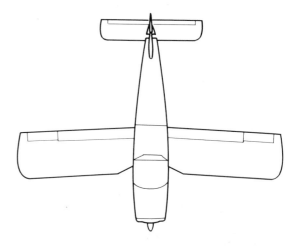

Span: 24.3 ft
Length: 19.2 ft
Height: 6.6 ft
Wing Area: 93 ft^2
Power: 0-200-A of 100 hp
Empty Weight: 750 lb
Useful Load: 520 lb
Gross Weight: 1270 lb
Stalling Speed: 50 mph
Cruising Speed: 135 mph

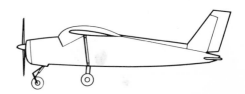

Barney Oldfield Aircraft Company
P. O. Box 5974
Cleveland, OH 44101

Andrew "Barney" Oldfield had long been an admirer of the Great Lakes Sport Trainer, so it was understandable that he decided to scale down this beautiful ship when he set out to design his first home-built. The Baby Lakes is a remarkable aircraft in that it is fully aerobatic and stressed for 9 Gs positive and negative. The plans were one of the first approved by the National Association of Aircraft Designers and enjoy the highest ratings applicable to a homebuilt design available to the builder. The plans and parts are now available through the engineering effort and coordination of Harvey R. Swack, shown in the accompanying photo.

Photo courtesy of Barney Oldfield Aircraft Company.

Harvey R. Swack, owner

Photo courtesy of
Harvey R. Swack.

Designation: Baby Lakes (Baby Great Lakes)
Seating: Single place
Type: Biplane
Aerobatic: Unlimited
Construction Material: Steel tubing, wood, fabric
Information Kit: $5
Plans Cost: $82 (Super Baby Lakes — 125 hp — $110)
Kits Available: For parts and welded components

Span: 16 ft 8 in
Length: 13 ft 6 in
Height: 4 ft 6 in
Wing Area: 86 ft^2
Power: 65 to 80 hp (Baby), 108 to 125 hp (Super)
Empty Weight: 480 lb
Gross Weight: 850 lb
Stalling Speed: 50 mph
Cruising Speed: 120 mph

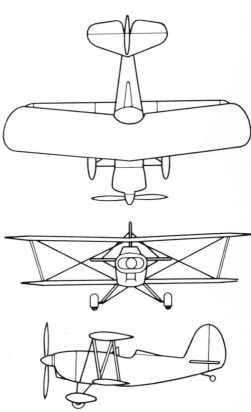

Bede Four Sales, Inc.
20340 North Benton Road West
North Benton, OH 44449

Jim Bede is well known as the designer of
the American Aviation two-place landplanes,
later produced by Grumman American, and
as designer of the BD-5 and BD-5J single-place
aircraft. While the future of the BD-5
program remains clouded, the BD-4 is a
successful design that has been built in
tricycle gear and tailwheel versions.

Designation: BD-4
Seating: Four place
Type: High-wing monoplane
Aerobatic: No
Construction Material: Aluminum alloy, fiber glass
Information Kit: $5
Plans Cost: $100 with builder's guide
Kits Available: For all parts

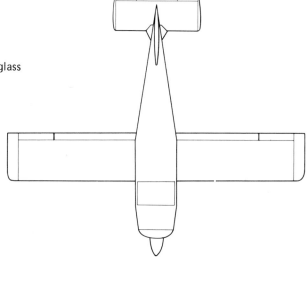

Span: 25 ft 7 in
Length: 21 ft 45 in
Wing Area: 102.3 ft^2
Power: 200 hp
Empty Weight: 1125 lb
Useful Load: 875 lb
Gross Weight: 2000 lb
Stalling Speed: 63 mph
Cruising Speed: 190 mph

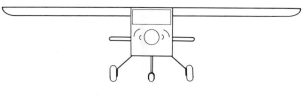

Peter M. Bowers
10458 16th Ave. South
Seattle, WA 98168

Peter Bowers is a well-known aeronautical engineer, aviation historian, and designer of homebuilt aircraft. Employed by Boeing Aircraft, Bowers originally designed the Fly Baby during 1954—1960 for competition in an EAA contest for low-cost, easily flown aircraft. Since that date, over 3800 sets of plans have been sold for single- and two-place monoplane and biplane versions.

Designation: Fly Baby (mono) and Bi-Baby (biplane)
Seating: Single and two side by side
Type: Monoplane or biplane
Aerobatic: Limited
Construction Material: Wood, fabric, aluminum leading edges
Information Kit: $2
Plans Cost: $60 for 200-pp book with biplane supplement
Kits Available: From various suppliers

Span: 28 ft
Length: 19 ft
Height: 6 ft
Wing Area: 120 ft^2 (monoplane)
Power: 65 to 100 hp
Empty Weight: 605 lb
Useful Load: 319 lb
Gross Weight: 924 lb
Stalling Speed: 42 mph
Cruising Speed: 90 mph

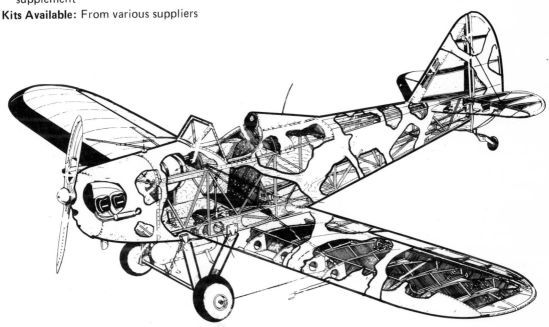

Brokaw Aviation, Inc.
2625 Johnson Point
Leesburg, FL 32748

Dr. Burgon Brokaw

Photo courtesy
of Brokaw
Aviation, Inc.

Photo courtesy of Brokaw Aviation, Inc.

Dr. Burgon Brokaw's interest in aircraft
dates back to 1938 when he won a Junior
Chamber of Commerce aviation contest
and started flying. The design of his Bullet
was initiated in 1966, with a first flight
realized during 1973. Structural design
and stress analysis was completed by
a professional engineer—Ernest R. Jones,
Ph. D. More powerful versions of the basic
design are being studied.

Designation: Brokaw Bullet
Seating: Two in tandem
Type: Low-wing monoplane
Aerobatic: Unlimited
Construction Material: All-metal stressed
   skin
Information Kit: $5
Plans Cost: $500 including construction
   manual and pilot's handbook
Kits Available: For components such as
   cowling, canopy glass, etc.

Span: 24 ft 1 in
Length: 23 ft 10 in
Height: 8 ft 10 in
Wing Area: 84.3 ft^2
Power: 310 hp
Empty Weight: 1933 lb
Useful Load: 1109 lb
Gross Weight: 3042 lb
Stalling Speed: 88 mph
Cruising Speed: 290 mph

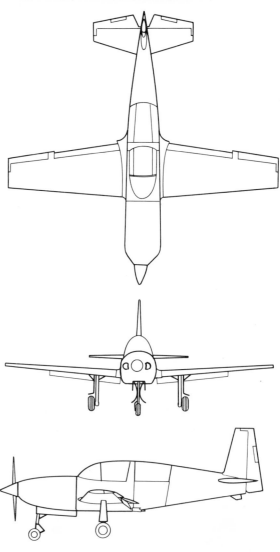

Bushby Aircraft, Inc.
Route 1 Box 13
Minooka, IL 60447

Midget Mustang I

The Midget Mustang was originally designed by David Long while he was chief engineer of Piper Aircraft. Completed in 1948, the prototype competed in the 1949 National Air Races and placed fourth in the Continental Trophy Race in Miami. The present versions of both the Midget Mustang and the Mustang II were developed by Robert Bushby, a research engineer with Sinclair Oil. Over 850 sets of Midget Mustang and 700 sets of Mustang II plans have been sold.

Designation: Model MM-1 Midget Mustang
Seating: Single place
Type: Low-wing monoplane
Aerobatic: Unlimited
Construction Material: All metal
Information Kit: $3
Plans Cost: $75
Kits Available: From the company

Span: 18 ft 6 in
Length: 16 ft 5 in
Height: 4 ft 6 in
Wing Area: 68 ft^2
Power: 85 to 135 hp
Empty Weight: 590 lb
Useful Load: 310 lb
Gross Weight: 900 lb
Stalling Speed: 57 mph
Cruising Speed: 240 mph

Designation: Model M-II Mustang II
Seating: Two side by side
Type: Low-wing monoplane
Aerobatic: Limited
Construction Material: All metal
Information Kit: $3
Plans Cost: $125
Kits Available: From the company

Span: 24 ft 2 in
Length: 19 ft 6 in
Height: 5 ft 3 in
Wing Area: 97 ft^2
Power: 160-hp Lycoming
Empty Weight: 927 lb
Useful Load: 573 lb
Gross Weight: 1500 lb

Midget Mustang II

Stalling Speed: 62 mph
Cruising Speed: 210 mph

Christen Industries, Inc.
1048 Santa Ana Valley Road
Hollister, CA 95023

After selling his successful equipment manufacturing company at an early age, Frank Christensen decided to focus his interest in aerobatics on developing a new competitive biplane. Along the way, he has also developed one of the most sophisticated line of construction kits available to homebuilders. The original single-place Eagle I has been modified to also provide the two-place Eagle II.

Designation: Eagle I
Seating: Single place
Type: Biplane
Aerobatic: Unlimited at competition weight
Construction Material: Steel tubing, wood, fabric
Information Kit: $10 (refunded with order)
Plans Cost: No plans — construction manuals with kits
Kits Available: Complete kits from company

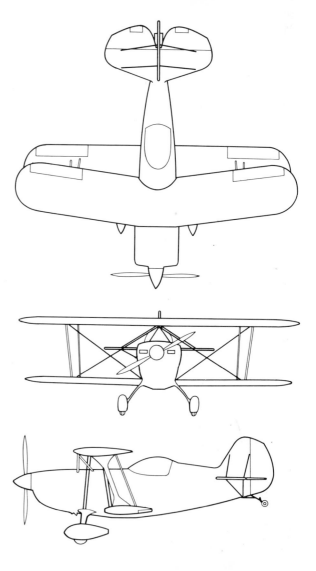

Span: 19 ft 11 in
Length: 18 ft 6 in
Height: 6 ft 6 in
Wing Area: 125 ft^2
Power: 260 hp
Weight: 997 lb
Useful Load: 481 lb
Gross Weight: 1478 lb
Stalling Speed: 56 mph
Cruising Speed: 165 mph

Note: The Eagle II is also available as a two-place tandem version of Eagle I

56

Anton Cvjetkovic
660 The Village No. 315
Redondo Beach, CA 90277

Photo courtesy of Anton Cvjetkovic.

Anton Cvjetkovic

Photo courtesy of
Anton Cvjetkovic.

Anton Cvjetkovic designed his first light airplane in 1951 when he was a member of the Zagreb Aero Club of Yugoslavia. After Cvjetkovic emigrated to this country in 1959, his subsequent light-plane designs included the CA-61, the CA-65 in wood, and the CA-65A of all-metal construction. With over 2000 sets of plans sold, many of these aircraft are under construction and flying at this time.

Designation: CA-65 and CA-65A Skyfly
Seating: Two side by side
Type: Low-wing monoplane (folding wing available)
Aerobatic: No
Construction Material: Wood (model CA-65) or all metal (CA-65A)
Information Kit: $5
Plans Cost: $125 (folding wing design $15 extra)
Kits Available: Not at present

Span: 25 ft
Length: 19 ft
Height: 7 ft 4 in
Wing Area: 108 ft^2
Power: 125 hp
Empty Weight: 900 lb
Gross Weight: 1500 lb
Stalling Speed: 55 mph
Cruising Speed: 155 mph

Note: Model CA-61 Mini Ace is also available

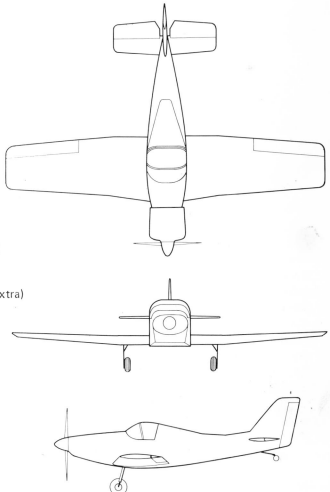

Nicholas E. D'Apuzzo
1029 Blue Rock Lane
Blue Bell, PA, 19422

Nick D'Apuzzo is a graduate aeronautical engineer with 42 years of active design experience, including project management for the Navy Bureau of Aeronautics, design of Goodyear class racing airplanes, and the development of a number of Naval aircraft. With continued assignments as a technical member of the United States Aerobatic Team, Nick's interest has focused on the design of successful aerobatic aircraft.

Photo courtesy of Nicholas E. D'Apuzzo.

Designation: Model D-260 Senior Aero Sport
Seating: Two in tandem
Type: Biplane
Aerobatic: Unlimited
Construction Material: Steel tubing, wood, aluminum sheet, fabric
Information Kit: $5
Plans Cost: $150
Kits Available: From the designer

Span: 27 ft
Length: 21 ft
Height: 7 ft 7 in
Wing Area: 185 ft^2
Power: 190 to 260 hp
Empty Weight: 1400 lb
Gross Weight: 2000 lb
Stalling Speed: 52 mph
Cruising Speed: 115 to 140 mph

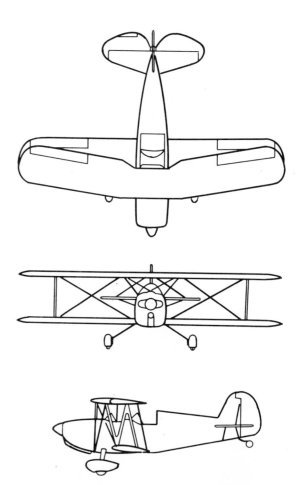

Note: Model D-201, an updated version of Model D-260, is also available

Leon D. Davis
Box 207
Stanton, TX 79782

Since Leon Davis is an aircraft mechanic specializing in experimental and prototype development, it is not surprising that his homebuilt design is of simple construction and can be built easily. This airplane is also quite efficient and reported to be flown easily.

Designation: Davis DA-2A
Seating: Two side by side
Type: Low-wing monoplane
Aerobatic: No
Construction Material: All metal
Information Kit: $3
Plans Cost: $120
Kits Available: Not at present

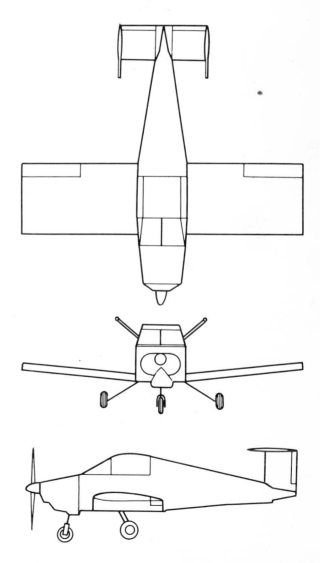

Span: 19 ft 3 in
Length: 17 ft 10 in
Height: 5 ft 5 in
Wing Area: 82.5 ft^2
Power: Continental A-65
Empty Weight: 620 lb
Gross Weight: 1125 lb

Stalling Speed: 60 mph
Cruising Speed: 110 mph

Durand Associates, Inc.
84th and McKinley Street
Omaha, NE 68122

Bill Durand

Photo courtesy of
Bill Durand.

Photo courtesy of Dick Stouffer.

The Mark V is fifth in the series of Durand
airplanes. Designer Bill Durand (EAA 31262)
is a registered professional engineer. During
15 years of teaching at the University of
Omaha, he headed the aeronautics unit of
the engineering department and served as
faculty sponsor of the University Flying
Club. Prior to forming a company to
develop the postwar XD-85 pusher, he was
a stress engineer with Martin-Nebraska Co.
during production of the B-29. In addition
to designing five small aircraft, he has
developed several other experimental
types either as analytical studies,
free-flight, or wind-tunnel models. This
research included rotors, canard, and low
aspect ratio wings of different plan forms.

Designation: Durand Mark V
Seating: Two side by side
Type: Biplane
Aerobatic: No
Construction Material: All metal
Information Kit: $5
Plans Cost: $150
Kits Available: Not at present

Span: 24 ft 6 in
Length: 20 ft 3 in
Height: 6 ft 8 in
Wing Area: 144 ft^2
Power: 150 hp
Empty Weight: 1210 lb
Useful Load: 630 lb
Gross Weight: 1840 lb

Stalling Speed: 60 mph
Cruising Speed: 135 mph

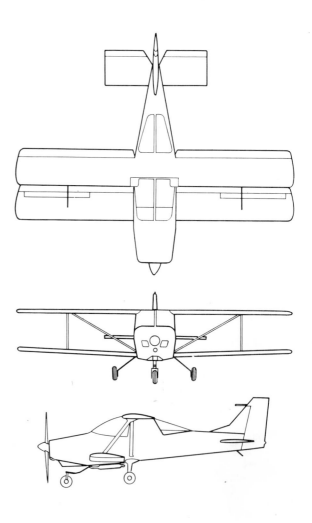

Evans Aircraft
P. O. Box 744
La Jolla, CA 92037

W. S. "Bud" Evans

Photo courtesy
of Evans Aircraft.

Photo courtesy of Evans Aircraft.

W. S. "Bud" Evans is a recently retired
aeronautical engineer who has over 30
years design engineering experience with
Ryan and Convair. As a result of this
structural background, nearly 6000 sets of
plans have been sold for the VP-1 and
VP-2 aircraft, with VPs flying in most
countries outside of the Iron Curtain.

Designation: VP-1
Seating: Single place
Type: Low-wing monoplane
Aerobatic: No
Construction Material: Wood, fabric
Information Kit: $3.50
Plans Cost: $75
Kits Available: From Stolp Starduster Corp.

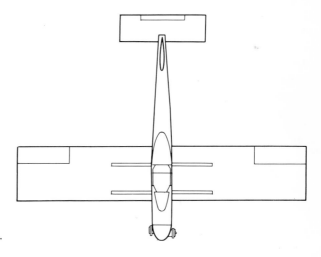

Span: 24 ft
Length: 18 ft
Wing Area: 100 ft^2
Power: 50 hp
Empty Weight: 440 lb
Gross Weight: 650 lb

Stalling Speed: 40 mph
Cruising Speed: 75 mph

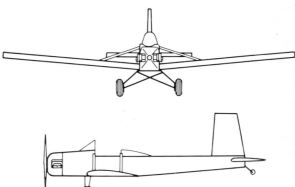

**Note: Model VP-2, a side-by-side two-seat version,
is also available**

William J. Fike
P. O. Box 683
Anchorage, AL 99510

Bill Fike is an experienced airline pilot and
mechanic who became sufficiently interested
in the advantages of STOL performance for bush
operation to develop the stall-resistant Model
E airplane. This design has also been successfully
adapted for radio-control models, indicating the
inherent stability of this airplane.

Photo courtesy of William J. Fike.

Designation: Fike Model E
Seating: Two in tandem
Type: High-wing monoplane (wing extensions
available)
Aerobatic: No
Construction Material: Steel tubing, wood, fabric
Information Kit: $5
Plans Cost: $37.50
Kits Available: Uses many standard production
aircraft parts

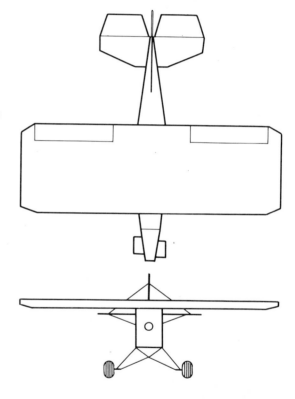

Span: 22 ft 4.5 in
Length: 19 ft 2 in
Height: 5 ft 8 in
Wing Area: 143.1 ft^2
Power: 85 hp
Empty Weight: 690 lb
Useful Load: 460 lb
Gross Weight: 1150 lb
Stalling Speed: 35 mph
Cruising Speed: 100 mph

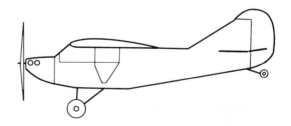

Javelin Aircraft Company, Inc.
1978 Easy Street
Wichita, KA 67230

Dave Blanton, president and chief design engineer of Javelin Aircraft, is an experienced aeronautical engineer with many design innovations to his credit. Well known to homebuilders for his experimental aircraft and engine developments, Dave has designed the Wichawk to FAA basic requirements around a ¾-scale Stearman trainer configuration.

Photo courtesy of Javelin Aircraft Company, Inc.

Designation: Wichawk
Seating: Two side by side
Type: Biplane
Aerobatic: Unlimited
Construction Material: Steel tubing, fabric
Information Kit: $5
Plans Cost: $125
Kits Available: From the company

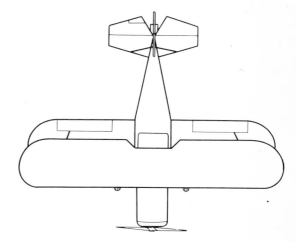

Span: 24 ft
Length: 19 ft 3 in
Height: 7 ft 2 in
Wing Area: 185 ft^2
Power: 125 to 200 hp
Empty Weight: 1280 lb
Useful Load: 720 lb
Gross Weight: 2000 lb

Stalling Speed: 48 mph
Cruising Speed: 135 mph

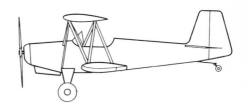

Jeffair
P. O. Box 975
Renton, WA 98055

Geoff Siers, designer of the Barracuda, was born and educated in England and served in the RAF as a fighter pilot. He has spent almost 17 years in various aspects of aircraft design, working on such airplanes as the BAC Lightning, the very advanced TSR-2 and the Concorde SST. In the United States he worked for 6 years with The Boeing Co. as a senior engineer. He and his family came to this country in 1964 and have lived in Washington state for the past 13 years. For the past 7 years he has been self-employed in his own very successful business and now does his engineering "purely for pleasure."

The Barracuda received the Most Outstanding New Design Award when first displayed at Oshkosh. Latest modifications include a larger engine and wing tip tanks.

Designation: Barracuda
Seating: Two side by side
Type: Low-wing monoplane
Aerobatic: No
Construction Material: Wood, fiber glass, some metal parts
Information Kit: $5
Plans Cost: $125
Kits Available: From Wick's Aircraft Supply

Span: 24 ft 9 in
Length: 21 ft 6 in
Wing Area: 120 ft^2
Power: 220 hp
Empty Weight: 1495 lb
Gross Weight: 2200 lb

Stalling Speed: 70 mph
Cruising Speed: 200 mph

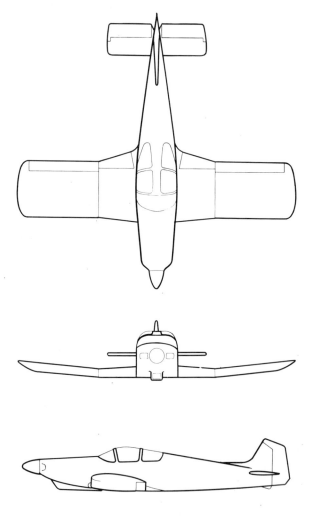

Jodel Aircraft (Avions Jodel)
36 Route De Seurre
21200 Beaune, France

Although his principal occupation now is aircraft company management and airplane construction, over the past 30 years J. Delemontez, president and director-general of Jodel, has developed numerous designs resulting in over 2000 homebuilt Jodel aircraft. Constructed mainly of wood, these proven designs are available in a number of single-seat, two-place, and three-passenger models.

Designation: D 92 Bebe
Seating: Single place
Type: Low-wing monoplane
Aerobatic: Limited at 500 lb weight
Construction Material: Wood with some metal parts
Plans Cost: 155 French francs
Kits Available: Not in U. S. at present

Span: 23 ft
Information Kit: $5
Length: 17.6 ft
Height: 4.5 ft
Wing Area: 97 ft^2
Power: 27- to 34-hp VW
Empty Weight: 350 lb
Useful Load: 250 lb
Gross Weight: 600 lb

Stalling Speed: 40 mph
Cruising Speed: 85 mph

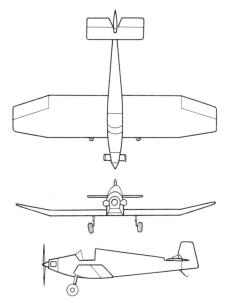

NOTE: Side-by-side two-seat Model D112 Club monoplane is also available

Designation: D 150 Grand Tourisme
Seating: Two side by side
Type: Low-wing monoplane
Aerobatic: No
Construction Material: Wood
Information Kit: $5
Plans Cost: 500 French francs
Kits Available: Not in this country

Span: 26.75 ft
Length: 20.33 ft
Height: 5.75 ft
Wing Area: 140 ft^2
Power: 100 Continental
Empty Weight: 920 lb
Useful Load: 670 lb
Gross Weight: 1590 lb

Stalling Speed: 55 mph
Cruising Speed: 135 mph

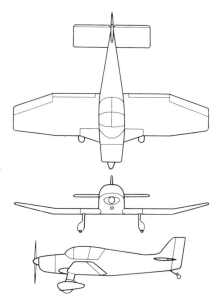

Note: The three-place Model DR 1050M is also available

Marcel Jurca (Colombes, Seine, France)
U.S. Representative: Kenneth Heit
581 Helen St., Mt. Morris, MI 48458

Marcel Jurca is an ex-military pilot and a hydraulics engineer who has been designing homebuilt aircraft since 1955. In addition to his original single- and two-place designs, Jurca has also developed a series of scaled-size World War II military fighter replicas. These aircraft and plans really require prior homebuilt experience and piloting skill ranging from average for the lighter aircraft to proficient for the World War II replicas.

Photo courtesy of R. A. Cole.

Designation: MJ-2 Tempete
Seating: Single place (two-seat version available in tandem)
Type: Low-wing monoplane
Aerobatic: Yes — inverted fuel system available
Construction Material: Wood, fabric
Information Kit: $3
Plans Cost: $150
Kits Available: Not available (55 aircraft flown by 6/80)

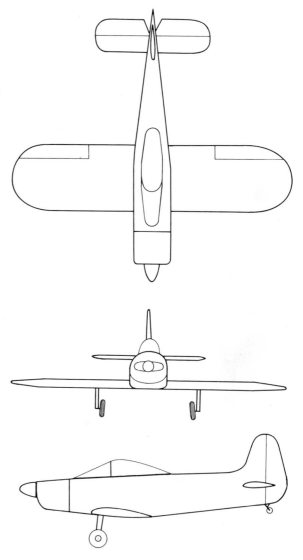

Span: 19 ft 6 in
Length: 19 ft
Height: 7.85 ft
Wing Area: 86 ft^2
Power: 65 to 180 hp
Empty Weight: 590 lb
Useful Load: 314 lb
Gross Weight: 904 lb
Stalling Speed: 50 mph
Cruising Speed: 125 mph

66

Marcel Jurca (cont'd)

Designation: MJ-3
Seating: Single place
Type: Low-wing monoplane
Aerobatic: Limited
Construction Material: Wood, fiber glass
Information Kit: $3
Plans Cost: $150
Kits Available: Not available at this time

Photo courtesy of Marcel Jurca.

Span: 19 ft 8 in
Length: 18 ft 8 in
Height: 7 ft 11 in
Wing Area: 95 ft^2
Power: 125 Lycoming
Empty Weight: 750 lb
Useful Load: 350 lb
Gross Weight: 1100 lb
Stalling Speed: 55 mph
Cruising Speed: 128 mph

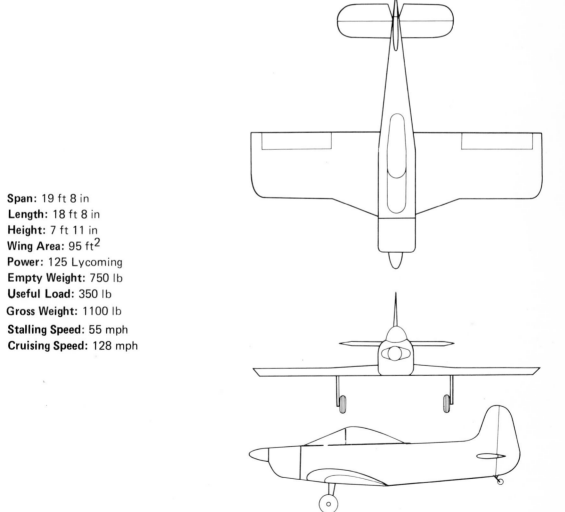

Marcel Jurca (cont'd)

Designation: MJ-5 Sirocco
Seating: Two in tandem
Type: Low-wing monoplane
Aerobatic: Limited
Construction Material: All wood (steel-tubing fuselage option)
Information Kit: $3
Plans Cost: $150 ($200 with steel-tubing fuselage)
Kits Available: Not available (30 aircraft flown by 6/80)

Photo courtesy of Marcel Jurca.

Span: 23 ft 4 in
Length: 20 ft
Height: 9 ft 5 in
Wing Area: 102 ft^2
Power: 115 to 200 hp
Empty Weight: 1250 lb
Useful Load: 400 lb
Gross Weight: 1650 lb

Stalling Speed: 55 mph
Cruising Speed: 150 mph

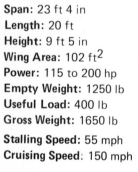

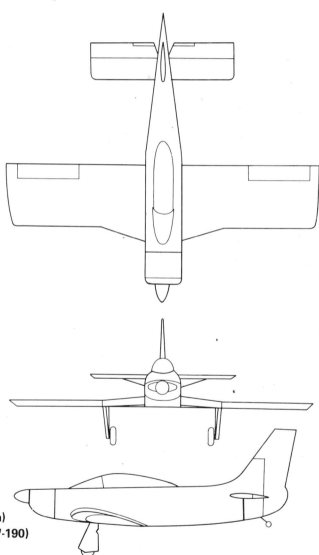

Note: MJ-7 Gnatsum (2/3-scale P 51 replica) and MJ-8 One-Nine-Oh (3/4-scale FW-190) are also available

**Dudley R. Kelly
Route 4
Versailles, KY 40383**

Designed by John Hatz, the first CB-1 was flown in 1968. Detail drawings for this airplane were made by Dudley Kelly who has since assumed responsibility for this program and also provides drawing sets for homebuilt construction. Kelly has now developed a new and equally easy to handle Model Kelly-D which may have either a steel-tubing or all-wood fuselage.

Designation: Hatz CB-1
Seating: Two in tandem
Type: Biplane
Aerobatic: Limited
Construction Material: Steel tubing, wood, fabric
Information Kit: $5
Plans Cost: $125
Kits Available: From approved sources

Span: 25 ft 4 in
Length: 19 ft
Height: 7 ft 10 in
Wing Area: 178 ft^2
Power: 100 hp
Empty Weight: 800 lb
Useful Load: 600 lb
Gross Weight: 1400 lb

Stalling Speed: 40 mph
Cruising Speed: 90 mph

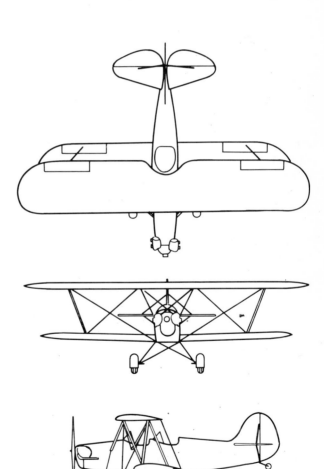

Dudley R. Kelly (cont'd)

Designation: Kelly-D
Seating: Two in tandem
Type: Biplane
Aerobatic: Limited
Construction Material: Steel tubing, wood,
   fabric (fuselage of steel tubing or wood)
Information Kit : $5
Plans Cost: $150
Kits Available: From approved sources

Span: 24 ft 4 in
Length: 19 ft 3 in
Power: 125 Lycoming 0-290-D
Empty Weight: 775 lb

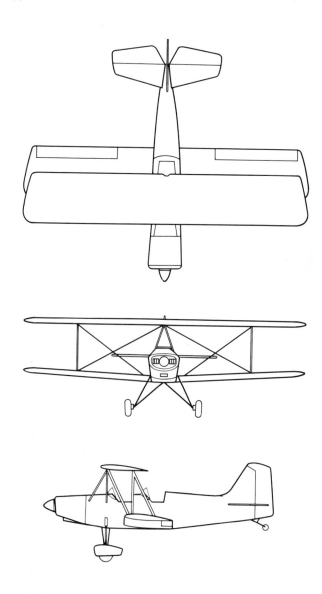

Edward Marquart
Box 3032
Riverside, CA 92519

Ed Marquart (EAA membership No. 198) has been designing and building pleasing biplanes for some time, and now offers two designs for homebuilders interested in sport flying and limited aerobatics.

Photo courtesy of Edward Marquart.

Designation: MA-5 Charger
Seating: Two in tandem
Type: Biplane
Aerobatic: Limited
Construction Material: Steel tubing, wood, fabric
Information Kit: $5
Plans Cost: $85
Kits Available: Some parts and assemblies available

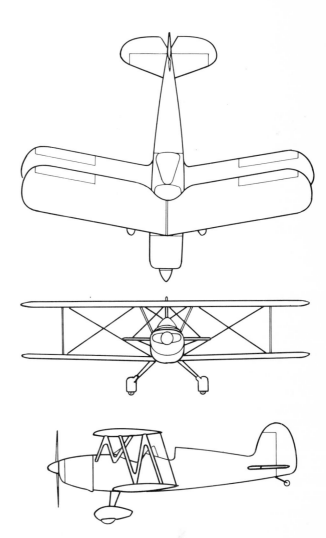

Span: 24 ft
Length: 19 ft 6 in
Height: 7 ft 6 in
Wing Area: 170 ft^2
Power: 100 to 180 hp
Empty Weight: 1000 lb
Useful Load: 550 lb
Gross Weight: 1550 lb

Stalling Speed: 42 mph
Cruising Speed. 115 mph

Note: MA-4 single-place
Lancer is also available

Monnett Experimental Aircraft, Inc.
955 Grace Street
Elgin, IL 60120

John T. Monnett has been designing high-performance, low-power aircraft to the racing monoplane Formula V rule since 1970. In addition, he has organized a plant to modify Volkswagen engines for aircraft and to produce parts for his designs, which currently include two powered landplanes, a sailplane, and a powered sailplane (see sailplanes for these).

Photo courtesy of Monnett Experimental Aircraft, Inc.

Designation: Sonerai I
Seating: Single place
Type: Mid-wing monoplane
Aerobatic: Unlimited
Construction Material: Steel tubing, sheet aluminum, fiber glass, fabric
Information Kit: $2
Plans Cost: $50
Kits Available: For parts, assemblies, raw materials, and hardware

Span: 16 ft 8 in
Length: 16 ft 8 in
Wing Area: 75 ft^2
Power: VW 1600 cc
Empty Weight: 440 lb
Useful Load: 310 lb
Gross Weight: 750 lb
Stalling Speed: 40 mph
Cruising Speed: 150 mph

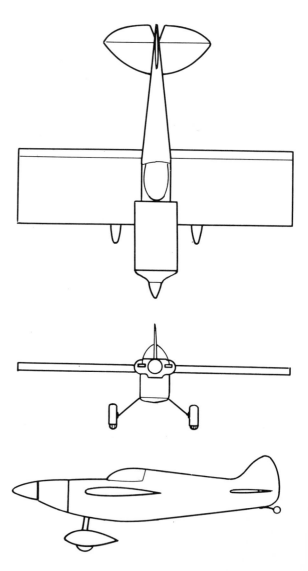

Note: Sonerai II, a two-place model, is also available

Pazmany Aircraft Corporation
Box 80051
San Diego, CA 92138

Ladislao Pazmany

Photo courtesy of
Warren D. Shipp.

Ladislao Pazmany received his aeronautical engineering degree in Argentina and has continued advanced studies at the University of California. His homebuilt designs are flown all over the world — Model PL-2 is used as a training plane by Nationalist China, Thailand, South Korea, and Indonesia. A design specialist with Convair and aerospace lecturer at the University of California, San Diego, Ladislao has designed numerous aircraft and written many books on aircraft design and construction.

Designation: PL-2
Seating: Two side by side
Type: Low-wing monoplane
Aerobatic: No
Construction Material: All metal
Information Kit: $5
Plans Cost: $150
Kits Available: From company and approved sources

Span: 28 ft
Length: 19.3 ft
Wing Area: 16 ft^2
Power: 108 to 150
Empty Weight: 902 lb
Gross Weight: 1447 lb
Stalling Speed: 52 mph
Cruising Speed: 132 mph

Photo courtesy of Pazmany Aircraft Corporation.

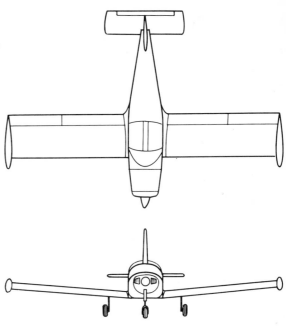

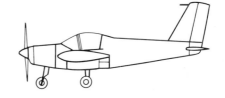

Pazmany (cont'd)

Designation: PL-4A
Seating: Single place
Type: Low-wing monoplane
Aerobatic: No
Construction Material: All metal
Information Kit: $5
Plans Cost: $100
Kits Available: From company and approved
　　　sources

Photo courtesy of Pazmany Aircraft Corporation.

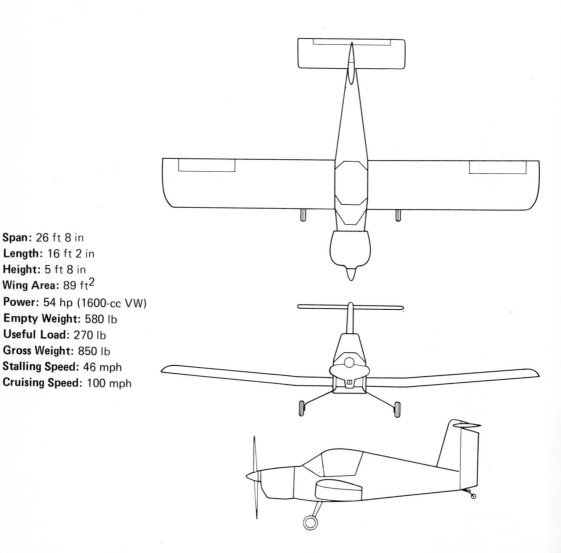

Span: 26 ft 8 in
Length: 16 ft 2 in
Height: 5 ft 8 in
Wing Area: 89 ft^2
Power: 54 hp (1600-cc VW)
Empty Weight: 580 lb
Useful Load: 270 lb
Gross Weight: 850 lb
Stalling Speed: 46 mph
Cruising Speed: 100 mph

Avions Claude Piel
c/o E. Littner, P. O. Box 272
Saint-Laurent, Quebec H4L 4V6, Canada

M. Piel's designs have been certified and produced in France for many years, one of the most notable being the CAP 10 developed from the homebuilt Emeraude airplane. Specializing in wood construction, Piel aircraft perform as nicely as they appear, owing to smooth surfaces and efficient design. Models currently available are listed.

Photo courtesy of Avions Claude Piel.

Designation: C. P. 60 series Diamant and Super-Diamant
Seating: 3 in Diamant, 4 in Super-Diamant
Type: Low-wing monoplane
Aerobatic: No
Construction Material: Wood, steel tubing, fabric
Information Kit: $5
Plans Cost: Contact E. Littner for version desired
Kits Available: Parts from approved sources

Span: 30 ft 6 in (Diamant)
Length: 21 ft 10 in
Height: 5 ft 10 in
Wing Area: 143.2 ft^2
Power: 100 to 115 hp
Empty Weight: 1020 lb
Gross Weight: 1740 lb
Stalling Speed: 60 mph
Cruising Speed: 115 mph

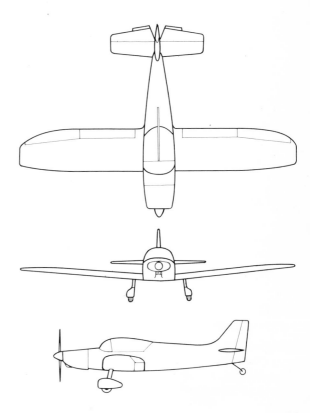

Piel (cont'd)

Photo courtesy of Avions Claude Piel.

Designation: C. P. 328 Super-Emeraude
Seating: Two side by side
Type: Low-wing monoplane
Aerobatic: Fully when flown solo
Construction Material: Wood, fabric
Information Kit: $5
Plans Cost: Contact E. Littner for version desired
Kits available: Parts from approved sources

Span: 26.5 ft
Length: 21 ft
Height: 8.3 ft
Wing Area: 117 ft^2
Power: 100 to 150 hp
Empty Weight: 850 lb
Gross Weight: 1540

Stalling Speed: 56 mph
Cruising Speed: 135 mph

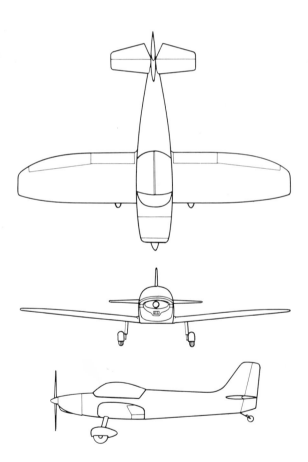

Note: Single-place Model C. P. 80 Zephyr monoplane and the tandem-seat Model C. P. 750 Beryl are also available

Pitts Aerobatics
P. O. Box 547
Afton, WY 83110

Designed by Curtis Pitts around the end of
World War II, the Pitts biplanes have long
been prominent in national and international
aerobatic competition, having at various
times held every major trophy. The design
is now under the direction of E. H. (Herb)
Anderson, Jr., with complete kits available for
homebuilders.

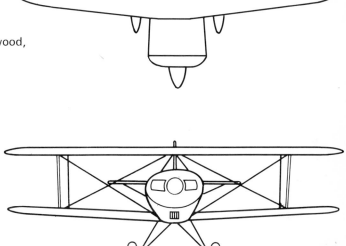

Designation: S-1D Special
Seating: Single place
Type: Biplane
Aerobatic: Unlimited
Construction Material: Steel tubing, wood,
  fabric
Information Kit: $7
Plans Cost: $150
Kits Available: Complete details and
  subassemblies

Span: 17 ft 4 in
Length: 5 ft 6 in
Height: 6 ft 3 in
Wing Area: 98.5 ft^2
Power: 180 hp
Empty Weight: 720 lb
Useful Load: 448 lb
Gross Weight: 1150 lb
Stalling Speed: 64 mph
Cruising Speed: 150 mph

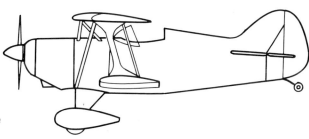

Note: Complete kit for S-1S single-place
      unlimited aerobatic biplane is
      available

Pitts Aerobatics (cont'd)

Designation: S-2 Series
Seating: Two in tandem
Type: Biplane
Aerobatic: Unlimited
Construction Material: Steel tubing, wood, fabric
Information Kit: $7
Plans Cost: Only with kit
Kits Available: Complete from company

Span: 20 ft
Length: 18 ft 3 in
Height: 6 ft 4 in
Wing Area: 125 ft^2
Power: 180 hp
Empty Weight : 900 lb
Useful Load: 600 lb
Gross Weight: 1500 lb

Stalling Speed: 58 mph
Cruising Speed: 140 mph

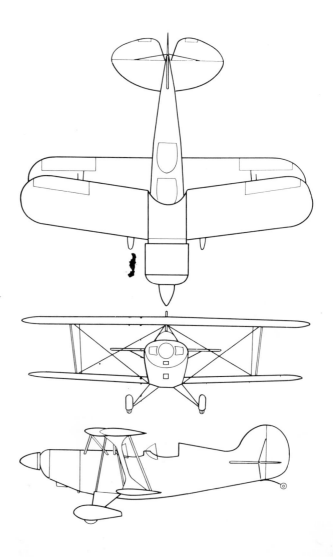

Practavia Ltd.
Wycombe Air Park
Booker, Bucks, England

In an effort to reduce the cost of owning an all-metal personal airplane, Brian Healey, an editor of British *Pilot* magazine, joined forces with Lloyd Jenkins and Peter Sharman of Loughborough University during 1969 to design and develop the two-place Sprite. Since then, about 150 of these aircraft have been started with a number now flying successfully.

Photo courtesy of Practavia Ltd.

Designation: Sprite
Seating: Two side by side
Type: Low-wing monoplane
Aerobatic: Unlimited when single place
Construction Material: All metal
Information Kit: $10 by air mail
Plans Cost: $150
Kits Available: Parts from the company

Span: 24 ft
Length: 19 ft
Height: 8 ft
Wing Area: 96 ft^2
Power: 125 hp
Empty Weight: 850 lb
Useful Load: 550 lb
Gross Weight: 1400 lb
Stalling Speed: 55 mph
Cruising Speed: 130 mph

Quickie Aircraft Corporation
P. O. Box 786
Mojave, CA 93501

Based on a concept for a minimum airplane originated by Tom Jewett and Gene Sheehan, as executed by Burt Rutan, the composite construction Quickie offers fast and efficient flying at minimum first and operating costs. Backed by a sophisticated builder's organization and complete kits, this airplane is reasonably simple to construct. However, the low power does not permit safe operation from short-length, grassy strips on hot days.

Designation: Quickie
Seating: Single place
Type: Tandem-wing airplane
Aerobatic: No
Construction Material: Composite foam, kevlar, fiber glass
Information Kit: $6
Plans Cost: $150
Kits Available: From company

Span: 16 ft 8 in
Length: 17 ft 4 in
Height: 3 ft 5 in
Wing Area: 55 ft^2
Power: 18 to 22 hp
Empty Weight: 240 lb
Useful Load: 240 lb
Gross Weight: 480 lb

Stalling Speed: 53 mph
Cruising Speed: 120 mph

Photo courtesy of Quickie Aircraft Corporation.

Rutan Aircraft Factory
Building 13 Mojave Airport
Mojave, CA 93501

As the result of his design experience with
aircraft spin characteristics at Edwards
Air Force Base, Burt Rutan realized the
importance of preventing wing stall to
preclude spinning. During the past 8
years he has developed a series of canard
aircraft offering stall-proof flight characteristics
when properly assembled and adjusted.

Photo courtesy of Rutan Aircraft Factory.

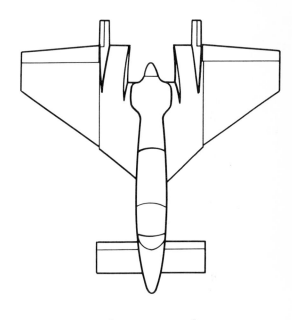

Designation: Vari Viggen
Seating: Two in tandem
Type : Canard
Aerobatic: No
Construction Material: Composite foam and
    fiber glass
Information Kit: $10
Plans Cost: $165
Kits Available: From approved sources

Span: 19 ft
Wing Area: 119 ft^2
Power: 150 hp
Empty Weight: 950 lb
Gross Weight: 1700 lb

Landing Speed: 55 mph
Cruising Speed: 155 mph

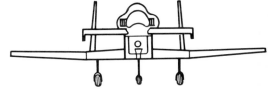

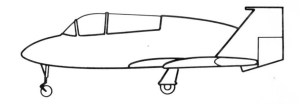

Rutan Aircraft Factory (cont'd)

Designation: VariEze and Long-EZ
Seating: Two in tandem
Type: Canard
Aerobatic: No
Construction Material: Composite foam and
    fiber glass
Information Kit: $5
Plans Cost: $139 to $212.50
Kits Available: Complete from approved
    sources

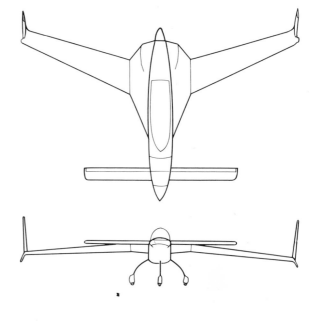

Span: 22.2 ft
Wing Area: 53.6 ft^2
Power: 100 hp
Empty Weight: 570 lb
Gross Weight: 1050 lb

Landing Speed: 70 mph
Cruising Speed: 170 mph

Sequoia Aircraft Corporation
900 West Franklin Street
Richmond, VA 23220

David B. Thurston

Sequoia Aircraft was founded by Alfred Scott, president, to provide a series of homebuilt aircraft offering superior performance plus design specifications approaching FAR Part 23 requirements. The Model 300 Sequoia and 302 Kodiak were designed by the author (David B. Thurston), while the F. 8L Falco wooden airplane was developed by Stelio Frati in Italy.

Designation: Model 300 Sequoia
Seating: 2 + 2
Type: Low-wing monoplane
Aerobatic: Unlimited at 2400 lb
Construction Material: All-metal wings and tail, steel-tubing fuselage, composite fuselage skin
Information Kit: $5
Plans Cost: $400
Kits Available: For complete airplane

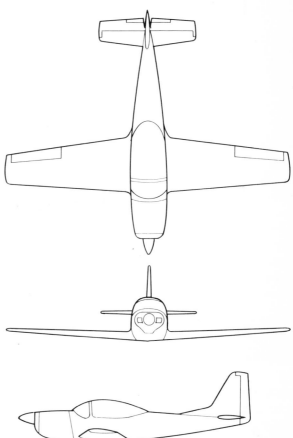

Span: 30 ft
Length: 25 ft
Wing Area: 130 ft^2
Power: 235- to 300-hp turbocharged
Empty Weight: 1800 lb
Useful Load: 1000 lb
Gross Weight: 2800 lb

Stalling Speed: 69 mph
Cruising Speed: 260 mph

Sequoia A/C (cont'd)

Designation: Model 302 Kodiak
Seating: Four place
Type: Low-wing monoplane
Aerobatic: Unlimited at 2400 lb
Construction Material: All-metal wings
and tail, steel-tubing fuselage, composite
fuselage skin
Information Kit: $5
Plans Cost: $400
Kits Available: For complete airplane

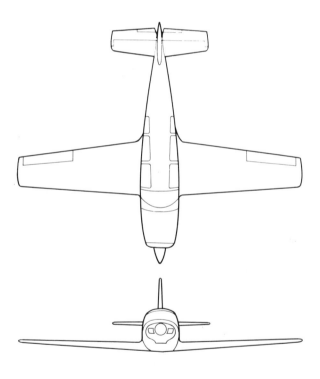

Span: 30 ft
Length: 25 ft
Wing Area: 130 ft^2
Power: 235- to 300-hp turbocharged
Empty Weight: 1850 lb
Useful Load: 1350 lb
Gross Weight: 3200 lb

Stalling Speed: 72 mph
Cruising Speed: 255 mph

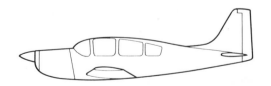

84

Sequoia A/C (Cont'd)

The F.8L Falco was designed by Stelio Frati who has an international reputation for such high-performance, light aircraft as the Aviamilano F. 250, SIAI Marchetti SF. 260 (used by the Waco meteor aerobatic team), and the F. 20 Pegaso twin-engine, six-place of 240 mph. S. Frati and D. Thurston assisted Alfred Scott in revising some of the F. 8L plans and simplifying some areas to permit use of U.S. standard parts and hardware (metric plans).

Courtesy of James Gilbert.

Designation: F.8L Falco
Seating: Two side by side
Type: Low-wing monoplane
Aerobatic: Unlimited
Construction Material: All wood
Information Kit: $10
Plans Cost: $400
Kits Available: For complete airplane

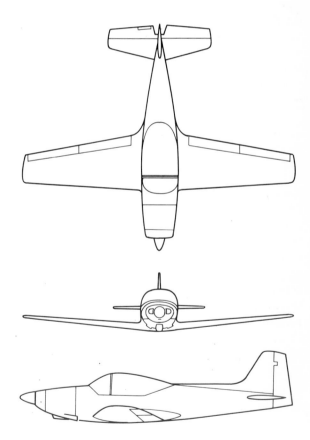

Span: 26 ft 3 in
Length: 21 ft 4 in
Height: 7 ft 6 in
Wing Area: 107.5 ft^2
Power: 135 to 160 hp
Empty Weight: 1010 lb
Useful Load: 530 lb
Gross Weight: 1540 lb
Stalling Speed: 58 mph
Cruising Speed: 180 mph

Sidewinder Corporation
P. O. Box 956
Temecula, CA 92390

Many Sidewinders have been flown since the prototype was completed in early 1969. Originally designed by Terry Smyth between 1958 and 1968, George Blair has since made this winner of the EAA 1969 Best Design Award relatively simple to build while providing efficient operation at a 160-mph cruising speed.

Photo courtesy of Sidewinder Corporation.

Designation: Sidewinder
Seating: Two side by side
Type: Low-wing monoplane
Aerobatic: Unlimited with an inverted fuel
    system
Construction Material: All-metal wings and
    tail surface, steel-tubing fuselage faired
    with aluminum alloy sheet
Information Kit: $5
Plans Cost: $125
Kits Available: From Wicks Aircraft,
    Aircraft Spruce and Specialty, and
    Sidewinder Corp.

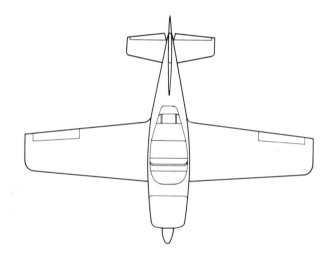

Span: 24 ft 10 in
Length: 19 ft 4 in
Height: 5 ft 5.5 in
Wing Area: 96 ft^2
Power: 125 hp
Empty Weight: 867 lb
Useful Load: 583 lb
Gross Weight: 1450 lb

Stalling Speed: 55 mph
Cruising Speed: 160 mph

Miniplane Smith's
3502 Sunny Hills Drive
Norco, CA 91760

Dorothy Smith

Photo courtesy
of Miniplane
Smith's

Designed for the amateur builder and pilot by
Frank W. Smith in 1956, this airplane has
been continued by his wife, Dorothy, and
son, Don, following Smith's death from a
heart attack. As of the spring of 1980, more
than 160 Miniplanes have been completed
and successfully flown.

Designation: Miniplane
Seating: Single place
Type: Biplane
Aerobatic: Unlimited
Construction Material: Steel tubing, wood,
    fabric
Information Kit: $1
Plans Cost: $25
Kits Available: For some parts

Span: Upper-17 ft, lower-15 ft 9 in
Length: 15 ft 1 in
Wing Area: 100 ft^2
Power: 65 to 125 hp
Empty Weight: 616 lb
Gross Weight: 1000 lb

**Note: Miniplane plus 1, a two-place model, is
    under development**

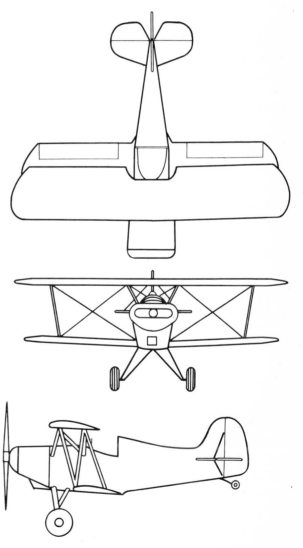

Sorrell Aviation
16525 Tilley Road South
Tenino, WA 98589

Based on a series of aircraft designed by
Hobie Sorrell, his three sons, John, Mark, and
Tim, formed Sorrell Aviation to market the
SNS-7 Hiperbipe, which developed from
the 1973 EAA Outstanding New Design
Award winning SNS-6. A fully aerobatic
airplane, the Hiperbipe is also an excellent
cross-country machine.

Photo courtesy of Jim Larsen.

Designation: Model SNS-7 Hiperbipe
Seating: Two side by side
Type: Negative-stagger biplane
Aerobatic: Unlimited
Construction Material: Steel tubing, wood,
   fabric
Information Kit: $7.50
Plans Cost: Only available with complete
   kits offered by the company

Span: 22 ft 10 in
Length: 20 ft 10 in
Height: 5 ft 10 in
Wing Area: 150 ft^2
Power: 180 hp
Empty Weight: 1236 lb
Useful Load: 675 lb
Gross Weight: 1911 lb

Stalling Speed: 49 mph
Cruising Speed: 160 mph

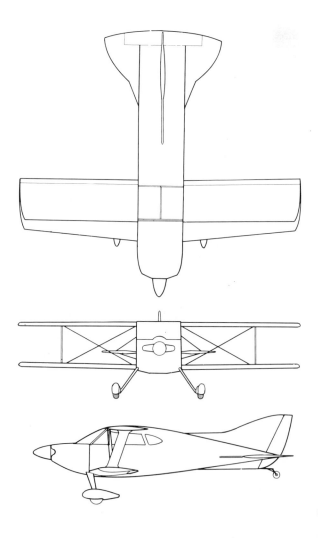

Steen Aero Lab, Inc.
15623 De Gaulle Circle
Brighton, CO 80601

The Skybolt was designed by Lamar
Steen, an aerospace science teacher in
Denver, between June 1968 and October
1970 when the prototype flew. This
airplane has been well received with
over 2000 sets of plans sold and many
successfully completed.

Designation: Skybolt
Seating: Two in tandem
Type: Biplane
Aerobatic: Unlimited
Construction Material: Steel tubing, wood,
    fabric
Information Kit: $5
Plans Cost: $50
Kits Available: From the company

Span: 24 ft
Length: 19 ft
Height: 7 ft
Wing Area: 153 ft^2
Power: 125 to 260 hp
Empty Weight: 1080 lb
Useful Load: 570 lb
Gross Weight: 1650 lb

Stalling Speed: 50 mph
Cruising Speed: 130 mph

Stewart Aircraft Corporation
11410 State Route 165
Salem, OH 44460

Donald Stewart designed the Headwind
in the early 1960s and first flew the prototype
during 1962. Between his airline flying duties,
Stewart has set up a company to provide
parts for the Headwind, as well as develop
this and other original aircraft models. The
Headwind prototype received the EAA
Best Auto Powered Design Award at
Rockford in 1962.

Designation: Headwind
Seating: Single place
Type: High-wing monoplane
Aerobatic: Limited
Construction Material: Steel tubing, wood,
  fabric
Information Kit: $5 with study prints
Plans Cost: $25
Kits Available: From the company

Span: 28 ft 3 in
Length: 17 ft
Height: 5 ft 9 in
Wing Area: 110.95 ft^2
Power: 53 hp
Empty Weight: 433 lb
Gross Weight: 700 lb

Stalling Speed: 40 mph
Cruising Speed: 85 mph

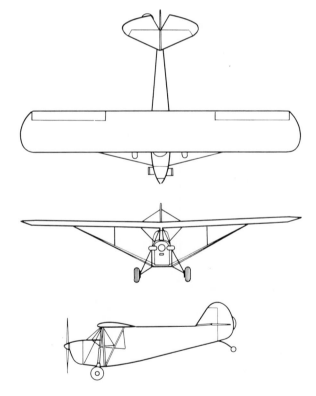

Stolp Starduster Corporation
4301 Twining, Flabob Airport
Riverside, CA 92509

Louis A. Stolp and George Adams designed a single-plane biplane named Starduster back in the late 1950s and have been at it ever since. Their well-known line of aircraft was acquired by Jim Osborne in 1972, although Lou Stolp, Vernon Payne, and many of the original members are still associated with aircraft developed by the company.

Designation: Starduster Too
Seating: Two in tandem
Type: Biplane
Aerobatic: Limited
Construction Material: Steel tubing, wood, fabric
Information Kit: $5
Plans Cost: $75
Kits Available: From the company

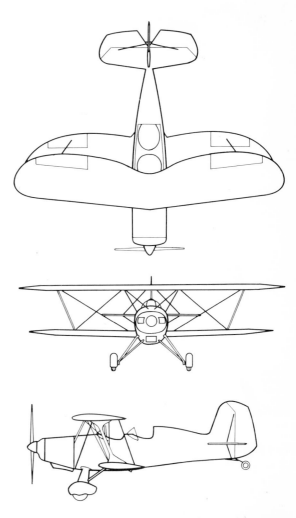

Span: Upper-24 ft, lower-20 ft 5 in
Wing Area: 162 ft^2
Power: 125 to 260 hp
Empty Weight: 1000 lb

Gross Weight: 1700 lb
Stalling Speed: 55 mph
Cruising Speed: 135 mph

Stolp (cont'd)

Designation: SA500 Starlet
Seating: Single place
Type: High-wing monoplane
Aerobatic: Limited
Construction Material: Steel tubing, wood, fabric
Information Kit: $5
Plans Cost: $50
Kits Available: From the company

Span: 19 ft
Length: 15 ft 9 in
Height: 6 ft 3 in
Wing Area: 105 ft^2
Power: 125 to 200 hp
Empty Weight: 740 lb
Useful Load: 450 lb
Gross Weight: 1190 lb

Stalling Speed: 55 mph
Cruising Speed: 90 mph

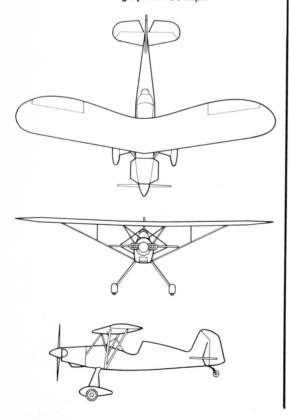

Designation: Model SA700 Acroduster I
Seating: Single place
Type: Biplane
Aerobatic: Unlimited
Construction Material: Aluminum alloy, wood, fabric
Information Kit: $5
Plans Cost: Available only with construction kit
Kits Available: For complete airplane

Span: 25 ft
Length: 17 ft
Height: 6 ft 8 in
Wing Area: 83 ft^2
Power: 108 hp
Empty Weight: 650 lb
Gross Weight: 1000 lb

Stalling Speed: 70 mph
Cruising Speed: 165 mph

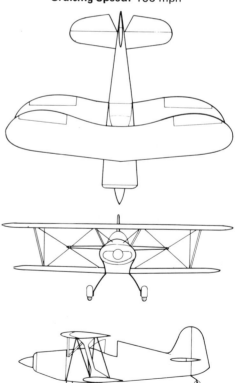

Stolp (cont'd)

Designation: Model SA750
    Acroduster Too
Seating: Two in tandem
Type: Biplane
Aerobatic: Unlimited
Construction Material: Steel tubing, wood,
, fabric
Information Kit: $5
Plans Cost: $75
Kits Available: From the company

**Note: Single-place biplane Model SA 900
V-Star is also available**

Span: 21 ft 5 in
Length: 18 ft 6 in
Height: 6 ft 10 in
Wing Area: 130 ft^2
Power: 200 hp
Empty Weight: 1050 lb
Useful Load: 750 lb
Gross Weight: 1800 lb

Stalling Speed: 60 mph
Cruising Speed: 150 mph

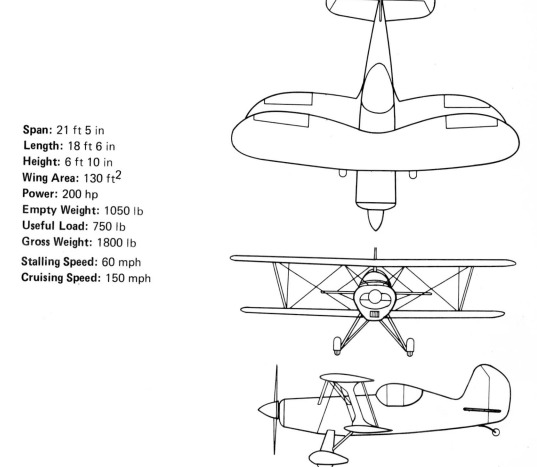

M. B. Taylor
P. O. Box 1171
Longview, WA 98632

Molt Taylor, an experienced aircraft designer, started his career developing special projects for the Navy during World War II. Following a series of radio-controlled targets, glide bombs, and similar programs, Molt developed the FAA-certified Aerocar. Among other projects he has more recently developed the Coot amphibian (see seaplanes) and Mini-Imp homebuilt designs.

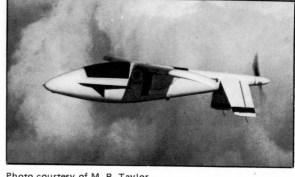

Photo courtesy of M. B. Taylor.

Designation: Mini-Imp
Seating: Single place
Type: Shoulder-wing monoplane
Aerobatic: No
Construction Material: Aluminum alloy,
   fiber glass
Information Kit: $5
Plans Cost: $200
Kits Available: From M. B. Taylor

Span: 25 ft
Length: 16 ft
Height: 4 ft
Wing Area: 75 ft^2
Power: 60 hp
Empty Weight: 500 lb
Gross Weight: 800 lb

Stalling Speed: 48 mph
Cruising Speed: 150 mph

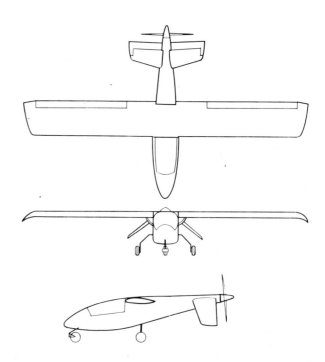

Thorp Engineering Company
P. O. Box T
Lockeford, CA 95237

John Thorp was employed by Lockheed during World War II as an aircraft design engineer, during which time he developed the Little Dipper and Big Dipper as well as the all-movable horizontal tail (stabilator). Since then he has participated in the design of the Fletcher FD-25, Derringer Twin, Volpar, and Piper Cherokee aircraft. His T-18 is one of the best-known homebuilt designs.

Designation: T-18
Seating: Two side by side
Type: Low-wing monoplane
Aerobatic: No
Construction Material: All metal
Information Kit: $5
Plans Cost: $180
Kits Available: From various suppliers

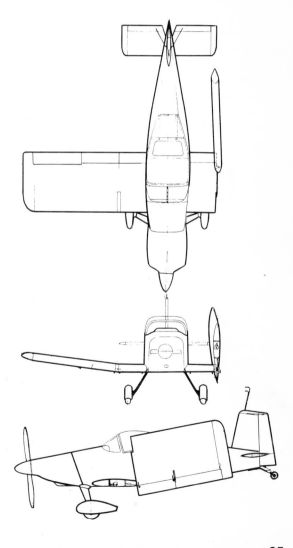

Span: 20 ft 10 in
Length: 18 ft 11 in
Height: 5 ft 1 in
Wing Area: 86 ft^2
Power: 125 hp
Empty Weight: 844 lb
Useful Load: 569 lb
Gross Weight: 1413 lb

Stalling Speed: 63 mph
Cruising Speed: 150 mph

Van's Aircraft
22730 SW Francis
Beaverton, OR 97005

Dick Van Grunsven

Photo courtesy of
Van's Aircraft.

Dick Van Grunsven is an experienced
aeronautical engineer who has developed
a series of high-performance, easily handled
aircraft. The prototype, RV-3, received
the EAA Best Aerodynamic Detailing
Award during the 1972 annual convention.
Since that time a large number of RV-3s
have been successfully completed, and
subsequent models have been developed.

Designation: RV-3
Seating: Single place
Type: Low-wing monoplane
Aerobatic: Limited
Construction Material: All metal
Information Kit: $3
Plans Cost: $85
Kits Available: From the company

Span: 19 ft 11 in
Length: 19 ft
Wing Area: 90 ft^2
Power: Lyc 0-290 G of 125 hp
Empty Weight: 695 lb
Gross Weight: 1050 lb
Stalling Speed: 48 mph
Cruising Speed: 180 mph

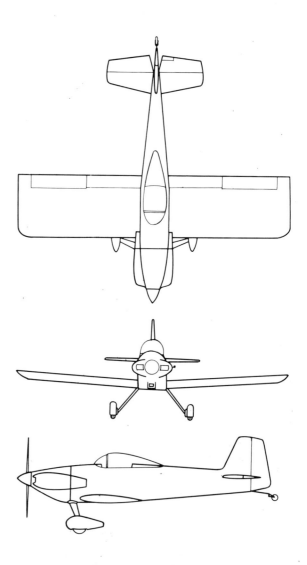

Van's A/C (cont'd)

Designation: RV-4
Seating: Two in tandem
Type: Low-wing monoplane
Aerobatic: Unlimited
Construction Material: All metal
Information Kit: $5
Plans Cost: Contact company
Kits Available: From company

Span: 23 ft
Length: 20 ft 4.5 in
Wing Area: 110 ft^2
Power: 150 hp
Empty Weight: 890 lb
Gross Weight: 1500 lb
Stalling Speed: 52 mph
Cruising Speed: 170 mph

Photo courtesy of Van's Aircraft.

Designation: RV-6
Seating: Two side by side
Type: Low-wing monoplane
Aerobatic: Limited
Construction Material: All metal
Information Kit: $5
Plans Cost: Contact company
Kits Available: From company

Span: 25 ft
Length: 20 ft 4 in
Wing Area: 115 ft^2
Power: 150 Lycoming
Empty Weight: 950 lb
Useful Load: 600 lb
Gross Weight: 1550 lb
Stalling Speed: 50 mph
Cruising Speed: 165 mph

Photo courtesy of Van's Aircraft.

Wag-Aero, Inc.
Box 181 1216 North Road
Lyons, WI 53148

In addition to providing parts for certified and homebuilt aircraft, Wag-Aero has developed two new kit designs based on early Piper aircraft models.

Designation: CUBy Sport Trainer
Seating: Two in tandem
Type: High-wing monoplane
Aerobatic: No (Acro Trainer model permits limited acrobatics)
Construction Material: Steel tubing, wood, fabric
Information Kit: Free
Plans Cost: $65 plus $18 for clipped wing (Acro) drawings
Kits Available: Complete from company

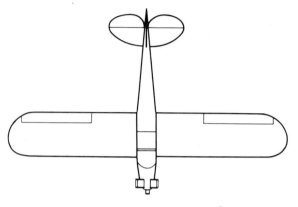

Span: 35 ft 2.5 in
Length: 22 ft 3 in
Wing Area: 178.5 ft^2
Power: 150 hp
Empty Weight: 720 lb

Useful Load: 680 lb
Gross Weight: 1400 lb
Stalling Speed: 39 mph
Cruising Speed: 94 mph

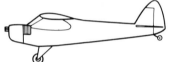

Designation: Wag-A-Bond (Classic and Traveler)
Seating: Two side by side
Type: High-wing monoplane
Aerobatic: No
Construction Material: Steel tubing, wood, aluminum alloy, fabric
Information Kit: Free
Plans Cost: $89
Kits Available: Complete from company

Stalling Speed: 45 mph
Cruising Speed: 100 mph

Span: 29.3 ft
Length: 18.7 ft
Height: 6 ft
Wing Area: 147.5 ft^2
Power: 65 to 100 hp (Classic)
Empty Weight: 640 lb
Gross Weight: 1250 lb

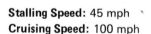

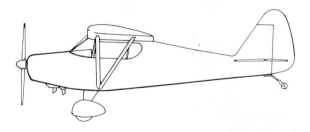

Gary Watson
Route No. 1
Newcastle, TX 76372

Gary Watson has developed the Windwagon to provide sport flying enthusiasts with an all-metal airplane of minimum weight. Assembly time is also a minimum if the complete kit (including engine) is used for construction of this new design.

Designation: Windwagon
Seating: Single place
Type: Low-wing monoplane
Aerobatic: No
Construction Material: All metal
Information Kit: $5
Plans Cost: $50
Kits Available: Complete from company

Span: 18 ft
Length: 12 ft 5 in
Height: 4 ft 2 in
Wing Area: 34 ft
Power: 35-hp VW
Empty Weight: 275 lb
Useful Load: 210 lb
Gross Weight: 485 lb
Stalling Speed: 40 mph
Cruising Speed: 100 mph

Western Aircraft Supplies
623 Markerville Road, N. E.
Calgary, Alberta T2E 5X1, Canada

Jean J. Peters, Glenn Gibb, and John Kopala joined forces (hence the "PGK" model designation) to design and develop the wood-and-fabric Hirondelle over a period of six years. In the process, some simplified construction methods have evolved which improve appearance and performance while reducing construction time.

Photo courtesy of Western Aircraft Supplies.

Designation: Model PGK-1 Hirondelle
Seating: Two side by side
Type: Low-wing monoplane
Aerobatic: No
Construction Material: Wood, fabric, some foam
Information Kit: $5
Plans Cost: Contact company
Kits Available: Complete from company

Span: 26 ft
Length: 20 ft 7 in
Height: 7 ft 6 in
Wing Area: 117 ft^2
Power: 115 hp
Empty Weight: 933 lb
Gross Weight: 1475 lb

Stalling Speed: 61 mph
Cruising Speed: 135 mph

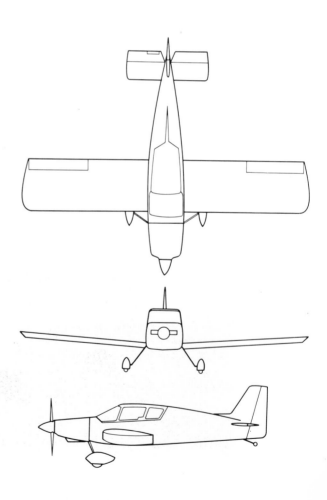

Steve Wittman
Box 2762
Oshkosh, WI 54901

No description of homebuilt aircraft could be
complete without Steve Wittman's aircraft.
Well known for his air race accomplishments
in the post-World War II Cleveland air races
and similar events, Wittman was one of
our first recognized homebuilder/designers.
As a result, he also became one of the founding
members of the EAA.

Designation: W-8 Tailwind
Seating: Two side by side
Type: High-wing monoplane
Aerobatic: Limited
Construction Material: Steel tubing, wood,
    fabric
Information Kit: $2
Plans Cost: $125
Kits Available: Not at this time

Span: 21 ft 11 in
Length: 19 ft 3 in
Height: 5 ft 3 in
Wing Area: 82 ft^2
Power: 135 hp
Empty Weight: 800 lb
Useful Load: 600 lb
Gross Weight: 1400 lb
Stalling Speed: 55 mph
Cruising Speed: 150 mph

Zenair Ltd.
236 Richmond Street
Richmond Hill, Ontario L4C 3Y8, Canada

Photo courtesy of Zenair Ltd.

Chris Heintz

Photo courtesy of Zenair Ltd.

Chris Heintz was born in France, received his aeronautical and design engineering degrees from E. T. H. Switzerland, worked on the Concorde at Aerospatial, and became chief engineer of Avions Pierre Robin. He and his family moved to Canada in 1973, where Zenair and the current line of homebuilt aircraft was started a year later. Operations since have been expanded to include manufacturing centers in Gainsville, Georgia and Seattle, Washington.

Designation: CH 100 Mono Z
Seating: Single place
Type: Low-wing monoplane
Aerobatic: No
Construction Material: All metal
Information Kit: $2
Plans Cost: $130
Kits Available: Complete from company

Span: 22 ft
Length: 19 ft 6 in
Height: 6 ft 6 in
Wing Area: 91 ft^2
Power: VW 1600 cc
Empty Weight: 580 lb
Useful load: 330 lb
Gross Weight: 910 lb
Stalling Speed: 47 mph
Cruising Speed: 105 mph

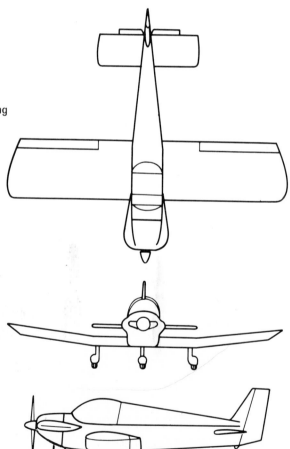

Zenair Ltd. (con'd)

Designation: CH 200 Zenith
Seating: Two side by side
Type: Low-wing monoplane
Aerobatic: Option available for aerobatic trainer
Construction Material: All metal
Information Kit: $3
Plans Cost: $170
Kits Available: Complete from company

Photo courtesy of Zenair Ltd.

Span: 23 ft
Length: 20 ft 6 in
Height: 6 ft 11 in
Wing Area: 105 ft^2
Power: 100 to 150 hp
Empty Weight: 900 lb
Useful Load: 550 lb
Gross Weight: 1450 lb

Stalling Speed: 53 mph
Cruising Speed: 150 mph

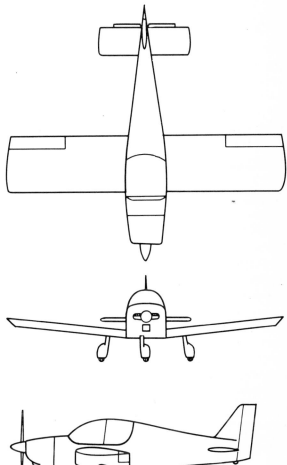

Note: Model CH 250 Zenith two-place side-by-side is also available with wing fuel tanks and the Model CH 300 rear window

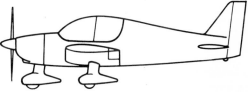

Zenair Ltd. (cont'd.)

Designation: CH 300 Tri Z

(3000-mile nonstop record set in July 1978)
Seating: Three place
Type: Low-wing monoplane
Aerobatic: No
Construction Material: All metal
Information Kit: $3
Plans Cost: $250
Kits Available: Complete from company

Photo courtesy of Zenair Ltd.

Span: 26 ft 6 in
Length: 22 ft 6 in
Height: 6 ft 10 in
Wing Area: 130 ft^2
Power: 125 to 180 hp
Empty Weight: 1050 lb
Useful Load: 750 lb
Gross Weight: 1800 lb

Stalling Speed: 53 mph
Cruising Speed: 145 mph

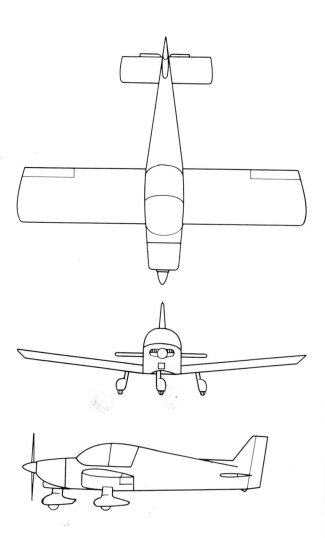

G. M. Zimmerman
8563 W. 68th Place
Arvada, CO 80004

The Akro was designed by C. L. Stephens
for homebuilders requiring a highly
competitive aerobatic airplane. First
flown in 1967, the Akro airframe is
stressed for +12 g and – 11 g. Data is
given for the Model B, which has an inverted
flight fuel and oil system, a constant speed
propeller, and a fuselage window below wings.

Designation: Stephens Akro Model B
Seating: Single place
Type: Mid-wing monoplane
Aerobatic: Unlimited
Construction Material: Steel tubing, wood,
fabric
Information Kit: $2
Plans Cost: $150
Kits Available: Not at this time

Span: 24 ft 6 in
Length: 19 ft 1 in
Height: 5 ft 9 in
Wing Area: 100 ft^2
Power: 180 Lycoming
Empty Weight: 950 lb
Useful Load: 350 lb
Gross Weight: 1300 lb
Stalling Speed: 55 mph
Cruising Speed: 160 mph

HELICOPTERS

At the present time there are a few helicopter designs marketed for homebuilt construction. All are two-place models, offering performance comparable to the recently certified Robinson R22 and having the same or similar power. The cost of building one of these models from the available kits will be about one-half to two-thirds the price of an R22. However, remember that in addition to the hours of construction and assembly time required for completion, a homebuilt helicopter will not have the market value of a certified production R22.

As an added note, the helicopter companies offer all builders and potential builders thorough flight instruction and checkout in flight-school machines, so it is possible to evaluate your interest and flight capability before deciding upon construction. With these basic thoughts, let us briefly review two homebuilt helicopters.

Hillman Helicopters, Inc.
P. O. Box 1411
Scottsdale, AZ 85252

The Hornet helicopter was designed by Doug Hillman who worked in Boeing's engineering department during the 1960s, winning many commendations, and the Pride in Excellence Engineering Award for tooling development and performance-oriented innovations. From Boeing, he went on to United Technology Center as senior systems analyst/engineer, in production of booster rockets for the Titan 3 Missile. Hillman founded Rotor Sport Inc. in 1973 to do research and development on the world's first Wankel Rotary Engine powered kit helicopter, the Wankelbee, which first flew July 1975. Moving facilities to Arizona in 1976, Hillman Helicopters, Inc. was founded and expanded at Falcon Field Airport near Mesa, Arizona, to promote production readiness of the all-new Hillman Hornet Helicopter, which first flew in September 1977. The Hornet won the Top Design Award at various air shows in 1978, including Best Operational Helicopter at Oshkosh.

Photo courtesy of Hillman Helicopters, Inc.

Photo courtesy of
Hillman Helicopters, Inc.

Doug Hillman

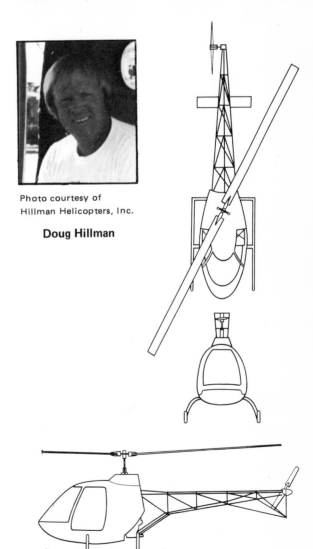

Designation: Hornet
Seating: Two side by side
Type: Single rotor, 2 blades
Aerobatic: No
Construction Material: Steel tubing, aluminum alloy blades, fiber-glass fairing
Information Kit: $10
Plans Cost: $100
Kits Available: Complete from factory

Power: Lycoming 0-320-A2B of 150 hp
Empty Weight: 800 lb (with body shell)
Useful Load: 600 lb
Gross Weight: 1400 lb
Cruising Speed: 90 mph

Rotor Way Aircraft, Inc.
14805 South Interstate 10
Tempe, AZ 85284

B. J. Schramm, designer of the Scorpion
133 and president of the company, began
his line of personal helicopter development
with the design of the Javelin back in 1958.
Since that time, B. J. has marketed the
single-place Scorpion, first flown in 1966,
and more recently the two-place Scorpion 133
which uses an engine developed by the
company.

Designation: Scorpion 133
Seating: Two side by side
Type: Single rotor, 2 blades
Aerobatic: No
Construction Material: Steel tubing,
    aluminum alloy blades, fiber-glass fairing
Information Kit: $5
Plans Cost: Available only with construction
    kit
Kits Available: Complete from factory

Power: 133 hp
Useful Load: 420 lb
Gross Weight: 1200 lb
Cruising Speed: 75 mph

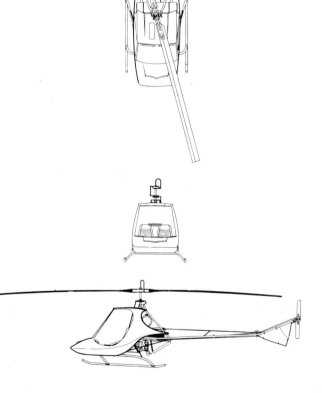

SAILPLANES AND GLIDERS

I have included powered and self-launching sailplanes in this category because they are *capable* of soaring without power. In addition to self-launching capability, the powered sailplane offers the convenience of returning to home base when thermal lift dies—saving the nuisance of dismantling and trailing home after the crew has located your landing position.

The various homebuilt sailplane designs and kits presented here include experimental types such as Al Backstrom's Flying Plank, offered by Vintage Sailplane Association; high-performance and very competitive 15-meter designs from Bryan Aircraft; and the Schweizer 2-33AK, the only FAA certified homebuilt kit currently available in the United States. In addition, an interested builder may select from previously noted power-assisted designs as well as relatively simple, rigid-frame construction hang gliders of both monoplane and biplane configuration, so if you are interested in building a glider or sailplane, the following selection contains something for everyone.

American Eagle Corporation
841 Winslow Court
Muskegon, MI 49441

Larry Haig designed and developed the
Eaglet to provide a simply built airframe offering
soaring performance comparable to the 1-26
and similar moderate glide ratio sailplanes. A
number of Eaglets have been completed and
successfully flown.

Designation: Eaglet
Seating: Single place
Type: High-wing monoplane powered glider
Aerobatic: No
Construction Material: Wood, metal, foam,
    fiber glass
Information Kit: $5
Plans Cost: $150 (refunded when kit completed)
Kits Available: From Aircraft Spruce &
    Specialty Co.

Span: 36 ft
Length: 16 ft
Height: 3 ft
Wing Area: 72 ft^2
Empty Weight: 160 to 170 lb
Useful Load: 200 lb
Gross Weight: 370 lb

Power: 12 hp
Stalling Speed: 38 mph
Max. Speed: 115 mph
L/D: 27:1

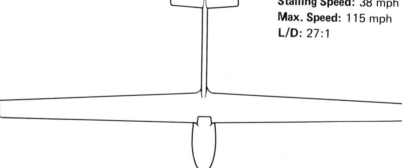

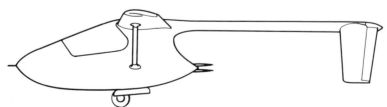

Bryan Aircraft, Inc.
Williams County Airport
Bryan, OH 43506

R. E. (Dick) Schreder is a well-known competition sailplane pilot and designer who has been active in this field for many years. Dick's designs are competitive with domestic and foreign models and offer the homebuilder the opportunity to own a high-performance sailplane at a reasonable price.

Note: Model RS15 single-place 15-meter sailplane is also available

Designation: HP 18
Seating: Single place
Type: Shoulder-wing 15-meter sailplane
Aerobatic: No
Construction Material: Aluminum alloy, foam, fiber glass
Information Kit: $5
Plans Cost: $150
Kits Available: From the company

Span: 49.2 ft
Length: 23.2 ft
Height: 4 ft
Wing Area: 113 ft^2
Empty Weight: 470 lb
Useful Load: 450 lb with ballast
Gross Weight 920 lb
Stalling Speed: 35 mph
Max. Speed: 150 mph
L/D: 40:1

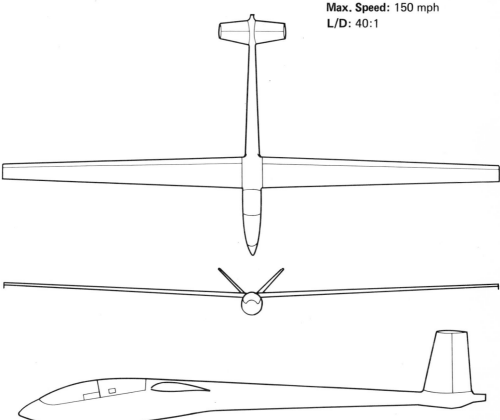

Designation: HP 19
Seating: Single place
Type: Shoulder-wing 15-meter sailplane
Aerobatic: No
Construction Material: Aluminum alloy, foam,
    fiber glass
Information Kit: $5
Plans Cost: $150
Kits Available: From the company

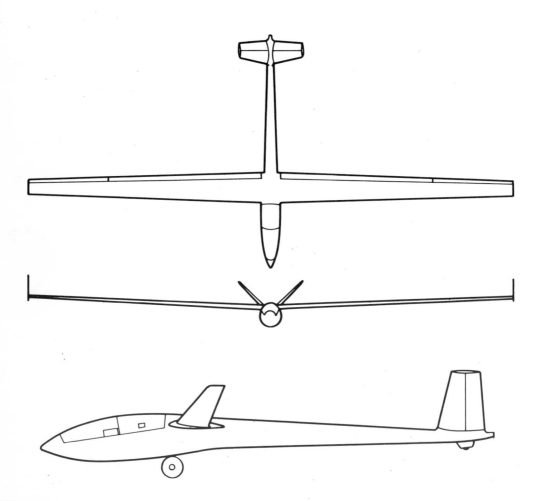

Monnett Experimental Aircraft, Inc.
955 Grace Street
Elgin, IL 60120

See Monnett Experimental Aircraft, Inc.
designs (landplanes) for background
information. The two sailplanes offered by
John Monnett have performance similar to
the Schweizer 1-26 and offer builders the
choice of pure soaring flight or power
assisted operation.

Designation: Monerai S
Seating: Single place
Type: Shoulder-wing sailplane
Aerobatic: No
Construction Material: Welded-tube fuselage;
    aluminum alloy tail boom, wings, and tail;
    fiber-glass fuselage fairing
Information Kit: $3
Plans Cost: With kit only
Kits Available: From company

Span: 36 ft
Length: 19 ft 7 in
Height: 2 ft 11 in
Wing Area: 78 ft^2
Empty Weight: 220 lb
Useful Load: 230 lb
Gross Weight: 450 lb

Stalling Speed: 38 mph
Max. Speed: 120 mph
L/D: 28:1

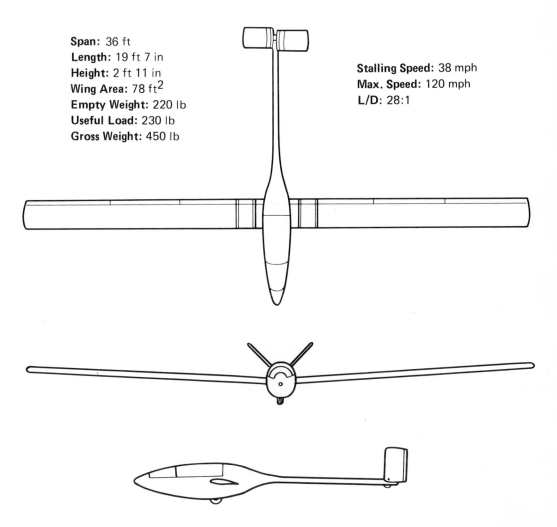

Designation: Monerai P
Seating: Single place
Type: Power assisted sailplane
Aerobatic: No
Construction Material: As for Monerai S
Information Kit: $3
Plans Cost: With kit only
Kits Available: From company

**Note: Specifications and performance
similar to Monerai S**

Schweizer Aircraft Corporation
Box 147
Elmira, NY 14902

The Schweizer family has been designing and manufacturing high-performance and training sailplanes for over 40 years. Their aircraft have held many national and international records during this period, with the Model 2-33 — the leading training sailplane in the U. S. — offered in kit form as a club trainer. When completed, this airplane will receive full FAA certification approval just the same as a factory-assembled production unit.

Photo courtesy of Schweizer Aircraft Corporation.

Designation: 2-33AK
Seating: Two in tandem
Type: High-wing monoplane
Aerobatic: No
Construction Material: Steel tubing, aluminum alloy, fabric
Information Kit: $2
Plans Cost: Not available separately
Kits Available: Complete from factory

Span: 51 ft
Length: 25 ft 9 in
Height: 9 ft 3.5 in
Wing Area: 219.5 ft^2
Empty Weight: 600 lb
Gross Weight: 1040 lb
Stalling Speed. 31 mph
Max. Speed: 98 mph
L/D. 23:1

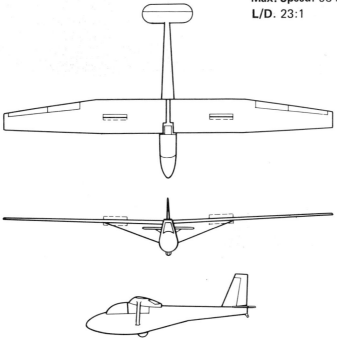

Vintage Sailplane Association
P. O. Box 301
Merrifield, VA 22116

Al Backstrom

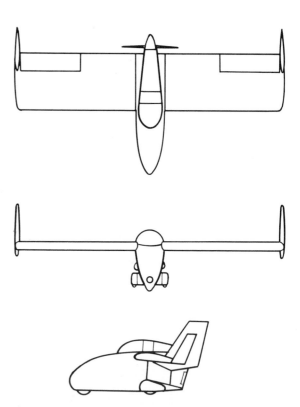

Photo courtesy of Al Backstrom.

Al Backstrom has been designing flying wing aircraft for the past 25 years, during which time he worked for the FAA in the southwestern region. His aircraft have been flying successfully all these years and have frequently participated in fly-bys at Oshkosh.

Designation: WPB-1 Flying Plank
Seating: Single place
Type: Power assisted flying wing sailplane
Aerobatic: No
Construction Material: Steel tubing, wood, fabric
Information Kit: $5
Plans Cost: $50
Kits Available: Not at this time

Span: 22 ft 2 in
Length: 11 ft 1 in
Wing Area: 97.5 ft^2
Power: 20 to 40 hp, two-cycle
Empty Weight: 340 lb
Useful Load: 220 lb
Gross Weight: 560 lb
Stalling Speed: 48 mph
Cruising Speed: 85 mph

Note: Plans for the unpowered Model EPB-1A Minimidget are also available

116

Volmer Aircraft
Box 5222
Glendale, CA 91201

Volmer Jensen

Photo courtesy
of Volmer Jensen.

Designation: VJ-11 Solo hang glider
Seating: Single place
Type: Biplane
Aerobatic: No
Construction Material: Wood, fabric, wire
    braced
Information Kit: $2
Plans Cost: $30
Kits Available: No

Volmer Jensen's interest in aviation preceded his flying as an aircraft carrier pilot during World War II. Since then he has been successfully engaged in manufacturing and engineering. Possibly best known for his VJ-22 Sportsman amphibian, the following model designations show Volmer's gliding interest dates back to 1940 and the VJ-11 program.

Span: 28 ft
Length: 15 ft 5 in
Height: 5 ft
Wing Area: 225 ft^2
Empty Weight: 100 lb
Useful Load: 180 lb
Gross Weight: 280 lb

Stalling Speed: 15 mph
Cruising Speed: 20 mph

Photo courtesy of Volmer Aircraft.

Volmer (cont'd)

Designation: VJ-23 Swingwing hang glider
Seating: Single place
Type: Monoplane
Aerobatic: No
Construction Material: Steel tubing, wood,
    fabric
Information Kit: $2
Plans Cost: $50
Kits Available: No

Note: Model VJ-23E, a powered version of
    Swingwing hang glider, and Model VJ-24,
    an unpowered version of Sunfun hang
    glider, are also available

Photo courtesy of Volmer Aircraft

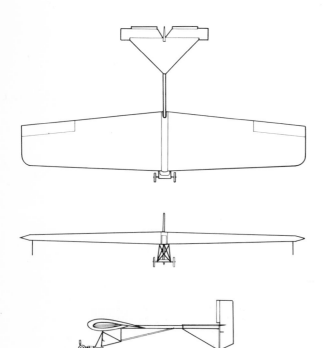

Span: 32 ft 7 in
Length: 17 ft 5 in
Height: 6 ft
Wing Area: 179 ft^2
Empty Weight: 100 lb
Useful Load: 200 lb
Gross Weight: 300 lb

Stalling Speed: 15 mph
Cruising Speed: 20 mph
L/D: 9:1

Volmer (cont'd)

Designation: VJ-24E powered Sunfun hang
    glider
Seating: Single place
Type: Monoplane
Aerobatic: No
Construction Material: Aluminum alloy tubing,
    fabric
Information Kit: $2
Plans Cost: $75 for engine installation only —
    Sunfun plans also required at $55
Kits Available: From the company

Span: 36 ft 6 in
Length: 18 ft 2 in
Height: 5 ft 8 in
Wing Area: 163 ft^2
Power: 10 hp
Empty Weight: 110 lb
Useful Load: 200 lb
Gross Weight: 310 lb

Stalling Speed: 15 mph
Cruising Speed: 20 mph
L/D: 9:1

Photo courtesy of Volmer Aircraft.

SEAPLANES

Flying from water or, better still, amphibious operation from land and water offers a level of sport flying and utility not possible from any other type of airplane. Unfortunately, some penalty is involved. Watercraft are heavier than landplanes of equivalent capacity because of the structure required to support water loads and are also slower for equivalent power because of the hull or floats hanging out in the breeze, but the added safety of being able to land on water or land in an emergency is a distinct amphibian asset not to be ignored. Not surprisingly, then, most of the seaplane designs available for homebuilt construction are amphibious.

Although all seven seaplanes reviewed here are hull types, it is worth noting that some landplane designs have been equipped with small twin floats; for example, Chris Heintz's two-place CH-200 Zenith has been successfully flown as a float seaplane.

With structures varying from wood and foam to steel tubing and fabric, fiber glass, or all-metal construction, one of the following combinations of materials and performance should suit most seaplane builders. The choice is yours!

Earl W. Anderson
4708 Arlington Road
Palmetto, FL 33561

Photo courtesy of Earl Anderson.

Earl Anderson

Photo courtesy
of Earl Anderson.

Some years prior to retiring as a Pan Am 747 captain, Earl Anderson designed, built, and flew the Kingfisher amphibian. Since 1970 about 200 sets of plans have been sold and 12 airplanes have been completed. If a builder wishes, metal spar J-3 Cub wings may be used to reduce construction time.

Designation: Kingfisher
Seating: Two side by side
Type: High-wing monoplane hull amphibian
Aerobatic: No
Construction Material: Wood, steel tubing, fabric
Information Kit: $5
Plans Cost: $150
Kits Available: Not at present

Span: 36 ft 1 in
Length: 23 ft 7 in
Wing Area: 185 ft^2
Power: 110 to 115 hp
Empty Weight: 1032 to 1075 lb
Useful Load: 468 to 575 lb
Gross Weight: 1500 to 1600 lb

Stalling Speed: 42 mph
Cruising Speed: 90 mph

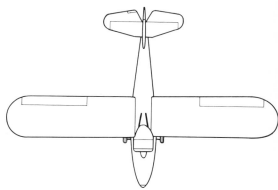
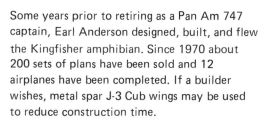

Osprey Aircraft
3741 El Ricon Way
Sacramento, CA 95825

George Pereira

Photo courtesy of Osprey Aircraft.

George Pereira, designer and builder of the Osprey, flew P-38s, B17s, and B29s during World War II and the Korean War. Following these years of service, he successfully designed and manufactured inboard power racing and ski boats. With this background, it is not surprising that George combined interests and developed the Osprey 1 and Osprey 2 amphibians. The Osprey 2 is currently offered, and a number of aircraft have been successfully flown.

Designation: Osprey 2
Seating: Two side by side
Type: Mid-wing monoplane hull amphibian
Aerobatic: No
Construction Material: Wood, foam, fiber glass
Information Kit: $5
Plans Cost: $150
Kits Available: From approved sources

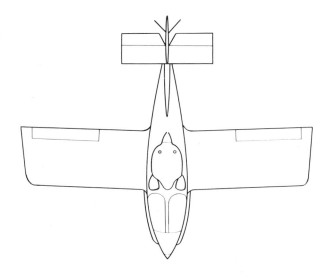

Span: 26 ft
Length: 21 ft
Height: 5 ft 8 in
Wing Area: 130 ft^2
Power: 150 hp
Empty Weight: 970 lb
Gross Weight: 1560 lb

Stalling Speed: 63 mph
Cruising Speed: 130 mph

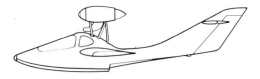

Spencer Amphibian Air Car
12780 Pierce Street
Pacoima, CA 91331

Photo courtesy of Don Dwiggins.

P. H. "Spence"
Spencer

Photo courtesy of
Don Dwiggins.

Everyone associated with water flying knows
P. H. "Spence" Spencer who was designing
and building seaplanes long before Republic
Aircraft produced a redesigned version of
his original and very clean Seabee amphibian.
Still flying and building in his eighties, Spence
offers the Air Car for homebuilders requiring
capacity and range.

Designation: S-12-E Air Car
Seating: Four place
Type: High-wing monoplane hull amphibian
Aerobatic: No
Construction Material: Wood, sheet metal,
    steel tubing, fiber glass
Information Kit: $5
Plans Cost: $195 with construction photos
    and specs
Kits Available: Complete from company

Span: 37 ft 4 in
Length: 26 ft 5 in
Height: 11 ft 9 in
Wing Area: 184 ft^2
Power: 260 to 285 hp
Empty Weight. 2150 lb
Useful Load: 1000 lb
Gross Weight: 3150 lb
Stalling Speed: 50 mph
Cruising Speed: 140 mph

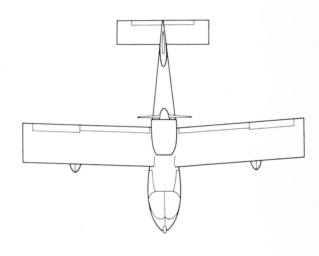

Spratt and Company, Inc.
P. O. Box 351
Media, PA 19063

Ever since his father assisted the Wright
brothers during their work at Kill Devil
Hill, George Spratt has been interested and
involved in aviation research and
development. His investigations have
resulted in a unique seaplane designed
around a pivoted wing control system
which cannot stall or spin. A few of
these airplanes have been built and
flown successfully.

Photo courtesy of Spratt and Company, Inc.

Designation: Control Wing
Seating: Two side by side
Type: High-wing monoplane flying boat
Aerobatic: No
Construction Material: Foam, wood, fiber
   glass
Information Kit: $5
Plans Cost: $150 with license to build
Kits Available: Not at this time

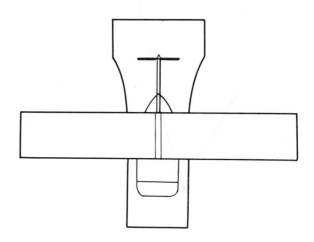

Span: 24 ft 4 in
Length: 17 ft 11 in
Height: 5 ft 2 in
Wing Area: 95 ft^2
Power: 60 to 85 hp outboard modification
Empty Weight: 500 lb
Useful Load: 500 lb
Gross Weight: 1000 lb

Cruising Speed: 80 mph

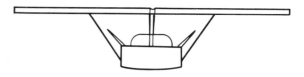

M. B. Taylor
P. O. Box 1171
Longview, WA 98632

See M. B. Taylor, p. 94.

Designation: Coot Amphibian
Seating: Two side by side
Type: Low-wing monoplane amphibian
Aerobatic: No
Construction Material: Wood, steel tubing,
   fiber glass
Information Kit: $5
Plans Cost: $150
Kits Available: From M. B. Taylor

Photo courtesy of M. B. Taylor.

Span: 36 ft
Length: 20 to 22 ft
Height: 8 ft
Wing Area: 180 ft^2
Power: 150 to 220 hp
Empty Weight: 1200 lb
Gross Weight: 1950 lb

Stalling Speed: 55 mph
Cruising Speed: 110 mph

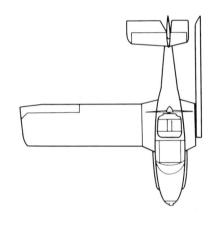

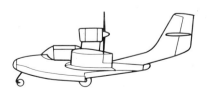

Thurston Aeromarine Corporation
16 Jericho Drive
Old Lyme, CT 06371

David B. Thurston

Photo courtesy of Kent Thurston.

David B. Thurston is a graduate aeronautical engineer who has been designing aircraft for over 40 years. His work has included fighter aircraft, guided missiles, and, for the past 25 years, light aircraft. Specializing in amphibian development, Thurston has designed the Colonial Skimmer (now the Lake Buccaneer), the Teal and the Trojan as well as conducting hydro-ski and hydrofoil aircraft research for the Naval Air Systems Command. He is the author of *Design for Flying* and *Design for Safety*.

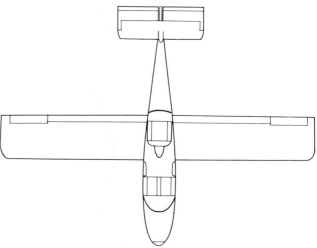

Designation: Model TA16 Trojan Amphibian
(3000 lb in Seafire version being FAA certified)
Seating: 2 to 4 place
Type: Shoulder-wing monoplane amphibian
Aerobatic: No
Construction Material: All-metal structure with fiber glass curved parts
Information Kit: Free leaflet for stamped envelope
Plans Cost: $550
Kits Available: Parts from approved sources

Span: 37 ft
Length: 27 ft 1.59 in
Wing Area: 183 ft^2
Power: 160 to 250 hp
Empty Weight: 1800 lb
Useful Load: 1200 lb
Gross Weight: 3000 lb

Stalling Speed: 57 mph
Cruising Speed. 145 mph

Volmer Aircraft
Box 5222
Glendale, CA 91201

See Volmer Aircraft, p. 117.

Designation: VJ-22 Sportsman
Seating: Two side by side
Type: High-wing monoplane amphibian
Aerobatic: No
Construction Material: Wood, steel tubing, fabric
Information Kit: $2
Plans Cost: $150
Kits Available: Aeronca wing panels used; certain parts from company

Photo courtesy of Volmer Aircraft.

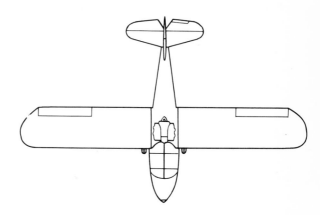

Span: 36 ft 6 in
Length: 24 ft
Height: 8 ft
Power: 100 hp
Empty Weight: 1000 lb
Useful Load: 500 lb
Gross Weight: 1500 lb

Stalling Speed: 45 mph
Cruising Speed: 85 mph

ULTRALIGHTS

Most of the very light aircraft collectively referred to as *ultralights* were originally developed as powered versions of hang gliders. However, this approach is now changing as the number of ultralights continues to grow at the fastest rate of any of the homebuilt types. As a result, many of the latest models have been designed as powered ultralights offering fuel economy, some range, and the opportunity to enjoy sport flying at minimum initial and operating costs.

Even though most of these aircraft have fixed landing gear, the FAA does not require that pilots of ultralights or their planes be licensed if the machines can be foot-launched and if operation is conducted within reasonable, proscribed limitations. The combination of relatively unrestricted flight and comparatively cheap aircraft kits has resulted in a boom in the ultralight industry. It is estimated that there are 20,000 such aircraft with some estimates reaching the heady (but exaggerated) height of 60,000 ultralights in current operation.

Because of the dynamic nature of this new dimension of homebuilt activity, it is impossible to include all the latest powered ultralights in a published text owing to the time required to complete the book; but a few of the 1980 models are reviewed here in order to present a cross section of these designs as well as indicate the type of flying offered by ultralight aircraft. The following 10 machines include models that have been flown across the country as well as some obviously developed from modified hang-glider designs; all are available in complete kit form, with a range of accessories offered by many suppliers.

Catto Aircraft
P. O. Box 1619
Cupertino, CA 95014

Craig Catto has developed a canard configuration offering low-speed flight at minimum weight. While not as simple in construction as some of the ultralights, this design has the capability of performing as a self-launched sailplane that can soar in thermal conditions.

Designation: Goldwing
Seating: Single place
Type: Canard ultralight
Aerobatic: No
Construction Material: Aluminum alloy
    tubing, foam, wood, mylar film
Information Kit: $5
Plans Cost: Only with kit
Kits Available: From company

Span: 36 ft
Wing Area: 119 ft^2
Power: 10 hp
Empty Weight: 95 lb
Gross Weight: 300 lb
Stalling Speed: 19 mph
Max. L/D 28:1 at 41 mph

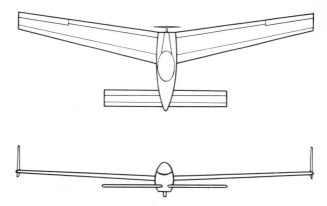

Franklin Manufacturing Corporation
R. D. 2
Glen Rock, PA 17372

Originally designed by Klaus Hill in 1977,
the Hummer was developed from Hill's
Superfloater glider. With many sailplane and
hang glider designs to his credit, Mr. Hill
has authorized Franklin Manufacturing
to produce and distribute the Hummer.

Designation: Hummer
Seating: Single place
Type: High-wing monoplane ultralight
Aerobatic: No
Construction Material: Aluminum alloy
    tubing, wire, fabric
Information Kit: $5
Plans Cost: Only with kit
Kits Available: From company

Span: 33 ft
Length: 18 ft
Height: 8 ft 3 in
Wing Area: 128 ft^2
Power: 20 to 25 hp
Empty Weight: 180 lb
Useful Load: 200 lb
Gross Weight: 380 lb
Stalling Speed: 20 mph
Cruising Speed: 30 mph

Mitchell Aircraft Corporation
1900 South Newcomb
Porterville, CA 93257

The Mitchell company has produced the
Mitchell Wing hang glider for some time,
having developed that design into the
B-10 foot-launched and tri-gear models.
With over 40 years of design experience,
Don Mitchell has now refined this flying-wing
configuration into the efficient Model U-2
Superwing which is capable of cruising at
60 mph on 10 hp.

Designation: Model U-2 Superwing
Seating: Single place
Type: Flying-wing monoplane ultralight
Aerobatic: No
Construction Material: Wood, foam, fiber
   glass, fabric
Information Kit: $6
Plans Cost: $95
Kits Available: Complete from the company

Span: 34 ft
Wing Area: 136 ft^2
Empty Weight: 145 lb
Useful Load: 210 lb
Gross Weight: 355 lb
Stalling Speed: 22 mph
Cruising Speed: 60 mph

Pterodactyl
847 Airport Road
Monterey, CA 93940

This new ultralight has been developed from a hang glider design equipped with an engine and tricycle landing gear. Two of these airplanes were flown from California to Oshkosh, Wisconsin in July 1979, climbing to clear mountain passes on the way.

Designation: Fledgling
Seating: Single place
Type: Flying-wing monoplane ultralight
Aerobatic: No
Construction Material: Aluminum alloy tubing, wire, fabric
Information Kit: $5
Plans Cost: Only with kit
Kits Available: From the company

Stalling Speed: 16 mph
Cruising Speed: 40 mph

Rotec Engineering, Inc.
P. O. Box 124
Duncanville, TX 75116

William Adaska

Photo courtesy
of William Adaska.

Photo courtesy of
Rotec Engineering, Inc.

Originally designed by Bob Lovejoy, the Quicksilver hang gliders have been developed into powered ultralights by William Adaska and his Rotec Engineering staff. In addition, John Mauro's successful Easy Riser has been given a propeller and is now offered as the Easy Riser power glider.

Designation: Rally 2 (formerly the powered Quicksilver)
Seating: Single place
Type: High-wing monoplane ultralight
Aerobatic: No
Construction Material: Aluminum alloy tubing, wire, fabric
Information Kit: $5
Plans Cost: Only with kit
Kits Available: Complete from company

Span: 32 ft
Wing Area: 160 ft^2
Power: 10.5 to 17 hp
Empty Weight: 115 lb

Stalling Speed: 16 mph
Cruising Speed: 30 mph

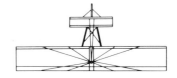

Designation: Powered Easy Riser
Seating: Single place
Type: Biplane tailless ultralight
Aerobatic: No
Construction Material: Aluminum alloy tubing, wire, fabric
Information Kit: $5
Plans Cost: Only with kit
Kits Available: Complete from company

Photo courtesy of Rotec Engineering, Inc.

Span: 30 ft
Wing Area: 170 ft^2
Power: 10 hp
Empty Weight: 90 lb
Useful Load: 200 lb
Gross Weight: 290 lb

Stalling Speed: 17 mph
Cruising Speed: 30 mph

Striplin Aircraft Corporation
P. O. Box 2001
Lancaster, CA 93534

After being involved in technical development projects and running his own small businesses, Ken Striplin turned to homebuilding as a hobby. A few aircraft later, he decided to develop and market a powered hang glider which has been developed into the tricycle landing gear, enclosed cabin Flac. A number of these aircraft have been built and flown successfully.

Photo courtesy of Striplin Aircraft Corporation.

Designation: Flac (foot-launched air-cycle)
Seating: Single place
Type: Flying-wing monoplane ultralight
Aerobatic: No
Construction Material: Wood, fiber glass, foam, fabric
Information Kit: $5
Plans Cost: Only with kit
Kits Available: Complete from company

Span: 32 ft
Length: 7 ft 7 in
Height: 4 ft
Wing Area: 155 ft^2
Empty Weight: 156 lb
Useful Load: 225 lb
Gross Weight: 381 lb

Stalling Speed: 20 mph
Cruising Speed: 50 mph

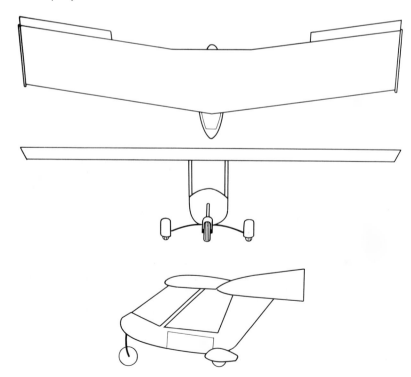

Ultraflight Inc.
6 George Street
Port Colborne, Ontario L3K 3S1, Canada

Dale Kramer designed the Lazair to provide low-powered, controlled flight. A unique system employs a single stick for pitch control and coordinated turns. The only twin-engine ultralight currently available, this design has received wide acceptance in the U.S. and Canada.

Designation: Lazair
Seating: Single place
Type: Twin-engine, high-wing monoplane ultralight
Aerobatic: No
Construction Material: Aluminum alloy tubing, foam, fabric
Information Kit: $5
Plans Cost: Only with kit
Kits Available: Complete from company

Span: 36 ft 4 in
Length: 14 ft
Height: 6 ft 4 in
Wing Area: 142 ft^2
Power: 11 hp (total from two engine)
Empty Weight: 135 lb
Useful Load: 215 lb
Gross Weight: 350 lb
Stalling Speed: 20 mph
Cruising Speed: 35 mph

Photo courtesy of Ultraflight, Inc.

Ultralight Flying Machines of Wisconsin
P. O. Box 248
Kansasville, WI 52139

John Moody of UFM is generally credited with being the first to successfully power a foot-launched ultralight. Since that development he has taken Larry Mauro's Easy Riser and added crosswind landing gear as well as the option of three different power packages to provide a powered ultralight airplane.

Designation: Powered UFM Easy Riser
Seating: Single place
Type: Biplane tailless ultralight
Aerobatic: No
Construction Material: Aluminum alloy
   tubing, wire, fabric
Information Kit: $5
Plans Cost: Only with kit
Kits Available: Complete from company

Span: 30 ft
Wing Area: 170 ft^2
Power: 10 to 15 hp
Empty Weight: 80 to 90 lb
Useful Load: 200 lb
Gross Weight: 290 lb

Stalling Speed: 17 mph
Cruising Speed: 30 mph

Photo courtesy of Ultraflight Flying Machines of Wisconsin.

John Moody

Weedhopper of Utah, Inc.
Box 2253
Ogden, UT 84404

John Chotia has designed more than 20
aircraft including hang gliders and powered
light aircraft. Construction of the
Weedhopper, his 24th design, began during
early 1978 and was completed by March
of that year. The latest, Model B, includes
many minor improvements incorporated
as the result of flight and service operation
of this successful design.

Designation: JC-24-B Weedhopper
Seating: Single place
Type: High-wing monoplane ultralight
Aerobatic: No
Construction Material: Aluminum alloy
   tubing, wire, fabric
Information Kit: $5
Plans Cost: Only with kit
Kits Available: Complete from company

Span: 28 ft
Length: 18 ft 6 in
Height: 6 ft 6 in
Wing Area: 168 ft^2
Power: 25 hp
Empty Weight: 160 lb
Useful Load: 220 lb
Gross Weight: 380 lb

Stalling Speed: 17 mph
Cruising Speed: 35 mph

Photo courtesy of Weedhopper of Utah, Inc.

At the risk of seeming repetitious, this is probably a good place to offer a few concluding thoughts about the homebuilt-aircraft available versus the type of airplane desired.

If you are primarily interested in sport flying, do you wish to fly cross-country in an open cockpit or in a heated cabin? Or does your preference lean toward aerobatic performance, possibly including air show work? Homebuilt aircraft can also be used for business trips, provided no one is carried for hire. Do you want an airplane primarily for fast travel and personal business? If so, one of the models designed for speed should be selected. Of course, there are also many subdivisions of this choice. Do you require short-field performance, or will your operations always be between surfaced runways over 3000 feet long? The difference lies in the relative safety of low landing speed for short runways versus higher cruising and landing speeds for faster travel—requiring longer runways.

One or more of the preceding designs should satisfy any of these criteria, so choose your airplane accordingly. But if you prefer a pioneer, antique, classic, replica, or custom model, move on to Chapter 7.

Pioneer, Antique, Classic, Replica, and Custom Aircraft

PIONEER, ANTIQUE, CLASSIC, AND REPLICA DESIGNS

Interest in finding and restoring old aircraft has long occupied the spare moments of many qualified pilots possessing some mechanical ability; possibly out of nostalgia for remembered days of leisurely flying or appreciation for some of the excellent design and construction details found on many early, practical aircraft. Certainly the short-field capability and the special enjoyment of open-cockpit flying offered by these older aircraft cannot be overlooked.

More and more homebuilder interest has recently focused on "the good old days" of aviation, with the result that increasing numbers of pilots are entering the restoration field as well as turning to the construction of replicas if the real thing is not available or cannot be found at an acceptable price.

Price is an important consideration for anyone interested in pioneer, antique, or classic restoration; in fact, both money and patience are needed. The purist will spend months or years going through old hangars and barns plus hours of correspondence to find an authentic replacement part. Building a new piece will only be considered as a last resort because the restored airplane should have all its original components, whenever possible, even to the same year of manufacture.

Such museum pieces are a delight to their owners and are sure to win the silver at fly-ins, but their cost is beyond the capability and interest of most people who would like to own an older airplane. Since Chris Sorensen and the editors of *Flying* magazine have covered this field most thoroughly in *Antique Airplanes* (see Ref. 7.1), the subject will not be further discussed here except to note that the high cost of pursuing an interest in authentic older aircraft has directed many homebuilders toward the replica market (see Figs. 3-2 through 3-5). As a result, a few replica plans and kits are now available, permitting you to assemble your own antique or classic airplane.

To go way back to the pioneer days, a replica of the original Scientific American Award–winning 1908 Curtiss June Bug, built by Joe Meade, president of Mercury Aircraft, and his associates at Hammondsport, New York, during 1975 and 1976, deserves an award for being the oldest design ever duplicated for actual flight as well as the most thoroughly researched flying replica ever built. Requiring some 4000

(a)

(b)

Figure 7-1 *(a)* Joe Meade at the wheel with the crew who built the Curtiss June Bug replica, Hammondsport, New York, June 1976. *(Courtesy of Pleasant Valley Wine Company.) (b)* Dave Fox flies June Bug II at Hammondsport, New York on June 23, 1976. *(Photo by Mike Mandiak, supplied by Joe E. Meade, Jr. of Mercury Aircraft.)*

hours of work to complete, the June Bug replica, with its 42.5-foot wingspan, was a sight to behold in flight. June Bug II, shown in Figure 7-1, was first flown for the public by Dave Fox on June 23, 1976, as part of Hammondsport's Bicentennial Celebration. This presentation honored Hammondsport as the "Cradle of Aviation" in commemoration of Glenn Curtiss's pioneer aircraft development and manufacture in this small town nestled at the foot of Keuka Lake. As a note of interest, anyone wishing to research early aircraft and engines should visit the Curtiss Museum, located in the center of Hammondsport. The files there contain sketches and patent application plans for many early Curtiss aircraft and engines as well as for those of other designers.

A later Curtiss replica is shown in Figure 7-2. This is a view of the "Great Race" recently held at the Owls Head Museum in Owls Head, Maine (near Rockland) between a 1911 Curtiss Pusher replica and an authentic Stanley Steamer (which was built in Maine). The Stanley Steamer can really go and proved a tough competitor for the Pusher, which has about the same takeoff, cruising, and landing speeds.

Another antique airplane, one that achieved unbelievable production for its time, is the Etrich Taube. This design is thoroughly researched and detailed in "Taube, Dove of War" (see Ref. 7.2). A replica of this 1912–1915 World War I airplane is now under construction for the Owls Head Museum at Rockland Airport and should be flying by the time this book is published. Since I provided volunteer engineering support for both the June Bug and Taube replicas, I can assure you that seeing one of

Figure 7-2 The "Great Race" between a Curtiss Pusher replica and an authentic Stanley Steamer at Owls Head Museum, Owls Head, Maine. *(From a color photo by Larry Shaw.)*

these old machines fly successfully provides a special thrill all its own, particularly when you were not sure just where the original designer wanted the center of gravity.

World War I replicas are becoming increasingly popular these days and may be found powered with their original engines for absolute authenticity or, more practically, with modern, certified, horizontally opposed, air-cooled engines. The Spad XIII in Figure 7-3, also flown at Owls Head Museum, is powered by a 4-cylinder Lycoming and, on occasion, may be seen dog fighting with a locally owned Fokker Dr. I triplane.

Jack Gardiner of Mill Valley, California, deciding that visibility was important in California's crowded skies, gathered data together and built a replica of the Royal Aircraft Factory 1915 Model Fighting Experimental 8 (F.E.8) pusher biplane shown in Figure 7-4. In order to provide a gun platform unobstructed by propeller rotation, the F.E.8 was designed with a 100-hp Gnome Monosoupape engine located in a pusher installation—offering excellent forward visibility as well as permitting the replica to be conveniently powered by a reliable 1967 145-hp Continental 0-300D engine. This airplane was flown from San Francisco to Rockland, Maine, during July 1980 and may now be seen in static and flight display at the Owls Head Museum along with some distinguished peers of the 1910–1920 era.

Plans for World War I airplanes can be found in the 1919 issue of Janes's *All the World's Aircraft,* by researching both in our National Air and Space Museum and in Europe (as was done for the Spad and Taube), or by purchasing drawings from the homebuilt suppliers reviewed farther along in this chapter.

Early aircraft books and special publications also offer authentic plans of antique

Figure 7-3   Spad XIII replica of Owls Head Museum, Owls Head, Maine. *(Steven Lang photo.)*

Figure 7-4 Jack Gardiner of Mill Valley, California, ready for takeoff in his Royal Aircraft Factory 1915 Model F.E.8 pusher biplane replica. Engine is a 145-hp Continental 0-300D. _(Photo by Toni R. Wight.)_

aircraft. A classic source is _Vehicles of the Air_ by Victor Lougheed, a founder of Lockheed Aircraft (see Ref. 7.3). If a copy of this text can be located by your library, it will prove to be a source for general arrangement drawings and construction details of the Montgomery gliders, Wright biplane, Antoinette monoplane, Curtiss biplane, Bleriot monoplane XI, Cody biplane, Farman Voisin biplane, and Santos-Dumont's Demoiselle monoplane, plus many pictures covering their engine installations and assembly. Such data provides a fine background for anyone wishing to construct a replica of one of these early machines.

For another approach to antique aircraft design data and plans, review old magazines such as the _Mechanical Package Magazine_ of the 1930s (see Ref. 7.5). For example, Volume I, Issues 2 and 3 of this magazine contain plans for machining a 2-cylinder, air-cooled airplane engine, Orville Hickman's Midget Seaplane, and a training glider. The 1931 edition of _Flying and Glider Manual_ contains drawings of the Curtiss Jenny, plans for a secondary glider and how to fly it, plans for Les Long's original Longster, the Drigg's Dart, the Church midwing Sport Monoplane, the Georgias Special, the Heath Seaplane Parasol plus its twin floats, and a glider motor conversion (see Ref. 7.4). These magazines of the 1930s contain a wealth of how-to-do-it data originated during a period when money was scarce and the homebuilt aircraft movement was just getting under way. Fortunately, we have always been blessed with aviation enthusiasts; if there wasn't money to buy it, they built it—and so, way back in the 1930s, the foundation was laid for today's EAA and homebuilding activity.

A few companies are now offering kits for antique homebuilt replicas ranging from World War I aircraft to versions of the Piper Cub (for example, Wag-Aero's Cuby and Wag-A-Bond models previously reviewed on page 98). Antique sailplane plans covering developments of the 1930s in this country and in Hitler's Germany have also recently become available. However, construction of these replicas should be undertaken only by those builders whose interest in gliding is combined with the ability to do fine woodworking at a level approaching the cabinetmaker's art. Their assembly requires time, patience, and the availability of fine veneers which are increasingly difficult to obtain (while rapidly becoming much more expensive than sheet aluminum alloy).

Although not complete, the following design review provides an indication of the type of replica plans and kits available for home construction. Unfortunately, such delightful airplanes as the Fairchild 22 or the various D.H. Moths and similar aircraft have not been offered to date but will probably become available for homebuilding as demand develops in the near future.

Redfern & Sons
Route 1 Box 98A
Athol, ID 83801

Data for these replica aircraft have been gathered in both the United States and Europe by Walter W. Redfern. Plans have been prepared from this material and have been altered from the original production drawings only as necessary to improve maintenance and initial assembly.

Photo courtesy of Redfern & Sons.

Designation: Fokker Dr-1 replica
Seating: Single place
Type: Triplane
Aerobatic: Limited
Construction Material: Steel tubing, wood, fabric
Information Kit: $4
Plans cost: $50 with construction photos
Kits Available: Not at present

Span: 23 ft 7 in
Length: 19 ft
Power: 150 hp
Wing Area: 205 ft^2
Empty Weight: 830 lb
Gross Weight: 1290 lb
Stalling Speed: 40 mph
Cruising Speed: 110 mph

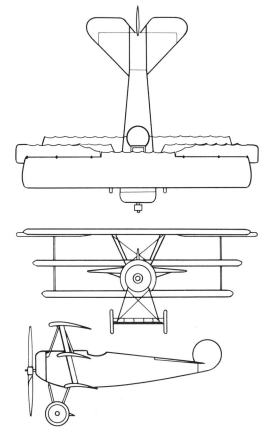

Note: Plans for a single-place replica of the World War I Nieuport 17 biplane are also available

Photo courtesy of Redfern & Sons.

Walter W. Redfern and some of his aircraft

Replica Plans
307 – 8680 Fremlin St.
Vancouver, B. C. V6P 3X3, Canada

Designation: SE-5A
Seating: Single place
Type: Biplane
Aerobatic: No
Construction Material: Wood with wire
    bracing, fabric covering
Information Kit: $5
Plans Cost $85
Kits Available: Not at present

Span: 23 ft 4 in
Length: 18 ft 2 in
Height: 7 ft 8 in
Wing Area: 146 ft^2
Power: Continental C85-12 (less electrics)
Gross Weight: 1150 lb

Stalling Speed: 35 mph
Cruising Speed: 85 mph

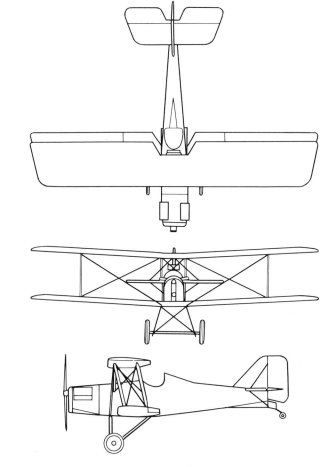

Vintage Sailplane Association
P. O. Box 301
Merrifield, VA 22116

Vintage Sailplane Association is a division of the Soaring Society of America. Archivist Bob Storck has gathered together one of the most complete sets of glider and sailplane records available today; of these, the following drawings are sufficiently complete to permit authentic homebuilt replica construction. Others will become available as the files continue to grow.

Photo courtesy of Geoff Steele.

Designation: Grunau Baby II
Seating: Single place
Type: High-wing utility glider (Germany, 1933)
Aerobatic: Limited — L/D = 18/1
Construction Material: Wood, fabric
Information Kit:
Plans Cost: $45 — English text
Kits Available: No

Note: Plans for the 1934 German Göppinger 1 Musterwolf and Hutter H-17, Single-place high-wing utility gliders, as well as the U. S. high-wing intermediate Rhonadler 32 sailplane are also available to qualified builders.

Empty Weight: 120 kg
Useful Load: 85 kg
Gross Weight: 205 kg

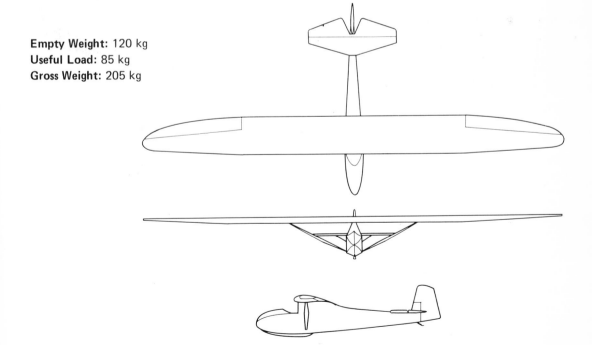

Vintage Sailplane Assoc. (cont'd).

Designation: Ross R-3
Seating: Single place
Type: Mid-wing sailplane (U.S., 1940)
Aerobatic: Limited — L/D approx. 30/1
Construction Material: Wood, fabric
Information Kit:
Plans Cost: $45
Kits Available: No

Span: 48 ft
Length: 20 ft 10 in
Wing Area: 132 ft^2
Empty Weight: 325 lb
Gross Weight: 550 lb

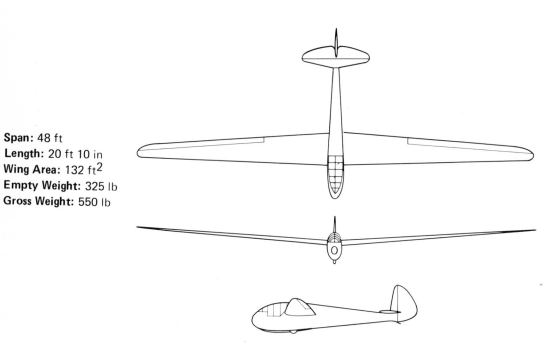

CUSTOM AIRCRAFT

The custom airplane, designed especially for one person to enjoy, probably represents the ultimate in homebuilding. Many owners achieve this goal by purchasing a set of standard plans and then modifying the configuration or cockpit area to suit their particular needs. The danger in doing this without first obtaining designer approval, of course, lies in the possibility of so changing the flight characteristics that operation becomes marginal or dangerous. As previously noted, if you plan to alter a standard design to obtain a custom airplane, be sure to obtain designer approval first or to incorporate his suggested methods of modification.

Some designers will not tolerate any changes in their aircraft for many reasons, including the special work involved on their part. When faced with this barrier to realizing a relatively easy path to a custom airplane, or when a very special design requirement and preference exists, the only alternative is to design and build a new airplane entirely from scratch (or, rather, from sketch).

To complete such a program successfully in minimum time and at reasonable cost, some experienced engineering advice and guidance is absolutely essential, not only to provide structural and aerodynamic design assistance but, equally important, to be sure the final design remains reasonably safe while satisfying your initial criteria.

Schatzie is such a custom airplane, designed and built by the owner, Charles D. Hoefelmann. Mr. Hoefelmann is executive vice president of Edo-Aire Mitchell, an autopilot company located in Mineral Wells, Texas. During the 9 years that Schatzie was under construction, and through various modifications and improvements such as retractable gear and increased power added since the first flight, all design and construction work was completed by the owner. As an insight to just how at least one custom airplane came into being, the following account has been graciously supplied by Mr. Hoefelmann for the benefit of all homebuilders; it is included here with appreciation for his dedication.

Designation: Schatzie
Seating: Two side by side

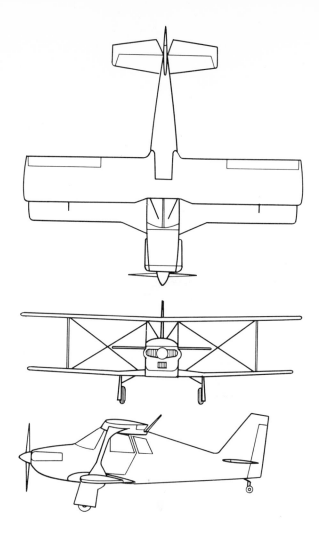

Span: 22 ft
Length: 18 ft 8 in
Height: 6 ft 8 in
Power: 150 hp
Gross Weight: 1680 lb

Cruising Speed: 138 mph
Landing Speed: 58 mph

Photo courtesy of Charles Hoefelmann.

Designing and building an airplane has always appealed to me as it does to most aviation enthusiasts. As the years passed and it became more feasible, the desire began to manifest itself more openly by a change in doodling habits from the customary geometric patterns to the narrow field of fuselage outlines and airfoil shapes.

Another telltale symptom was an intense interest in the far corners of repair shops where broken and bent pieces of airplanes are found in various stages of nudity; there to study the size, shape, and function of the inner workings, storing ideas for future reference. This seems to be a very necessary process for would-be designers who lack engineering knowledge—much less the ability to help Number One Son with eighth-grade math.

While the desire to build was progressive in nature, the actual decision to build and final commitment to action came with a degree of suddenness. The moment was precipitated one balmy February evening in Phoenix in 1958 when increasing self-reproach for the wasteful use of television as panacea for the pressures of business was eclipsed by the desire to build.

Immediate action followed, and by late evening an unidentified airfoil shape was laid out on the back of two calendar sheets taped end to end. The cord was 38 in. (length of two calendar sheets) and the thickness ratio, it later developed, was about 13 percent. The precise contour of the airfoil was scientifically established by bending a kite stick to an aesthetic curve. Admittedly, model building in the teens and a stint as an A&E in earlier years contributed to an otherwise offhand approach to the airfoil shape.

The next night, the airfoil was transferred to a rib jig on a flat board. This was done by placing the original layout sheets on the board and nailing the jig blocks in place. By the end of the evening, the original document was lost forever, having been torn off in pieces.

During the next 3 weeks, 44 ribs were built, and some basic conclusions about the rest of the airplane were made.

In the beginning, I had no idea that Schatzie would be a reverse stagger wing biplane in the classic form of the Beech Model 17. I did know that it would be a biplane. This decision was reached early and necessitated by the inherent strength of this configuration versus a lack of ability to engineer a cantilever design. Besides, there is always the nostalgic appeal of the biplane. The enclosed cabin was another firm decision, the rationale being that by the time it was finished, I would no longer care to have my gray hair whipped by the wind in an open cockpit. Then, too, I had been somewhat spoiled by the convenience of modern electronics and instrumentation. I wanted the room for such things and room for baggage so that it would be a useful and practical machine.

A bit of doodling with the weight and balance factors soon confirmed that a conventional wing stagger was impractical. Even after reversing the stagger, it was necessary to shoulder the upper wing at the root in order to get a reasonable windshield slant and a desirable profile.

Work progressed slowly and intermittently over the 9-year construction period. The last part of building any airplane is always the hardest; the tasks of building molds for the nose cowl and windshield, then finishing the engine baffling, electrical wiring, the interior, etc., etc. This was also a period when the least amount of spare time was available for the project.

Finally, in early 1967, there was nothing left to do but see if it would fly. You don't think about this question much during construction, when all your thoughts are absorbed in design details and you work with complete confidence that it will. After all, that's the purpose of the whole exercise. But sometime during the few final steps, the question does occur briefly as though it was never there before.

Final inspection, temporary certification, and the official christening were all completed, but the first test-flight awaited weather improvement. When the time did come, there was only one friend on hand to observe. This was because I didn't want the pressure of an audience and because on this day I did not intend to do more than taxi runs and short lift-offs to feel things out. After a few taxi runs, I began to make short lift-offs. Just as I was about to throttle back on about the third or fourth run, the urge struck, and off we went to circle the patch. This was an exhilarating moment, to say the least.

Upon landing, the usual smiles and jokes prevailed: "How'd it fly?" "I dunno, help me pry my fingers from these controls!"

I regret that there are no plans available for those who have asked. Everything is done on an eyeball basis, and the few notes and scribbles that were made would be of little use to anyone. Being like the house that Jack built, it is a bit overweight and complex, with tubes running every which way. Anyone who wanted to build a similar design could best start from scratch.

Be these shortcomings as they may, when you are zinging along with a tail wind on some purposeful trip and you look out at those stubby little wings you built yourself, you get a feeling that can only come one way. So if you enjoy building, get yourself a couple of old calender sheets, a kite stick, and a pencil.

Note the "if" in the preceding paragraph. It's important. To repeat the admonition of other builders and designers, if you are looking for a low-cost airplane to get into the air and your interests are largely in flying, go rent an airplane from the nearest FBO; it's cheaper and quicker. If you enjoy creative handwork, have an understanding family, and are willing to spend almost every spare minute of your time on a project, you will be richly rewarded.

When your aviation interest can only be satisfied by building a custom design—a "one-only" airplane in the world—our flight regulations will fortunately permit you to do so. Just realize that some degree of professional aircraft design assistance is mandatory and that a considerable span of time will pass before the first takeoff; but that first flight in your own special airplane will make it all worthwhile, as Charlie Hoefelmann and many others have learned over the years.

REFERENCES

7.1 Chris Sorensen, *Antique Airplanes*, Scribner, New York, 1979.

7.2 Col. John A. De Vries, "Taube, Dove of War," *Historical Aviation Album*, P.O. Box 33, Temple City, CA 91780, 1978.

7.3 Victor Lougheed, *Vehicles of the Air*, The Reilly and Britton Company, Chicago, 1911.

7.4 *Flying and Glider Manual*, Fawcett Publications, Minneapolis, 1931.

7.5 *Mechanical Package Magazine*, Fawcett Publications, Minneapolis, 1932.

Powerplant Selection

Although I personally prefer a certified production engine, many homebuilt aircraft are successfully flown with automotive and small, 2-cycle engines. In fact, some very recent conversions of these engines are quite efficient, so sophisticated that they are capable of operating as long as 2000 hours between overhauls. However, the cost of modified powerplants is rapidly approaching that of certified engines, a fact that certainly tends to eliminate any price advantage anticipated from automotive power. When combined with certain negative aspects of automobile engines—single ignition, main bearings and crankshafts designed for medium-power operation, extremely high revolutions per minute (rpm) for full power, basically heavy design, plus the possible bother of a water-cooling system—the advantages of using an automotive-type powerplant should be carefully studied before making a final decision. Nonetheless, we shall take a look at some of these converted powerplants after discussing the certified, horizontally opposed engines.

CERTIFIED ENGINES

Over the years, I have frequently been asked which engines are installed in the various production airplanes so that an interested builder might locate a wreck having a usable engine of the type desired. Hopefully such wrecks are few and far between but engines do run out and are removed from time to time. In such cases, they may be purchased fairly reasonably and then locally overhauled at a considerable saving over a factory remanufactured or overhauled engine. Also, if you should fly an airplane with a particularly satisfying powerplant while looking for an engine for your new homebuilt, it would be most helpful and convenient if you could determine the engine model for that airplane. With this in mind, the following tables, though not covering every horizontally opposed engine, have been included to narrow that search and provide specifications for your new homebuilt powerplant.

Another interesting source of engine versus airplane installations will be found in *General Aviation Engine Suspensions* (see Ref. 8.1). This 90-page manual also contains shock mount suspension drawings and data for numerous reciprocating and turbine engine installations found on general aviation aircraft and is therefore a doubly useful powerplant reference.

TABLE 8-1 Continental Engines

MODEL	NO. of CYL.	TAKEOFF POWER HP@RPM	METO POWER HP@RPM	BORE & STROKE	DISP. CU/IN	ENGINE DIMENSIONS LENGTH	WIDTH	HEIGHT	WEIGHT DRY LBS. BASIC ENG.	PROP. DRIVE	FUEL GRADE	COMP. RATIO
0-200	4		100-2750	4.06 x 3.87	200	28.50	31.56	23.18	188	Direct	80/87	7.0:1
0-300-A* & C*	6		145-2700	4.06 x 3.87	300	39.75	31.50	23.25	270	Direct	80/87	7.0:1
0-300-D*	6		145-2700	4.06 x 3.87	300	36.00	31.50	27.00	272	Direct	80/87	7.0:1
IO-360-A*,C*,D*,G*, & H* †	6		210-2800	4.44 x 3.87	360	34.60	31.40	24.33	294	Direct	100/130	8.5:1
IO-360-J*,JB	6	210@2800	195-2600	4.44 x 3.87	360	34.60	31.40	24.33	294	Direct	100/130	8.5:1
IO-360-K*,KB	6		195-2600	4.44 x 3.87	360	34.60	31.40	24.33	294	Direct	100/130	8.5:1
TSIO-360-A*	6		210-2800	4.44 x 3.87	360	35.84	33.03	23.75	300	Direct	100/130	7.5:1
TSIO-360-C*,CB	6		225-2800	4.44 x 3.87	360	35.84	33.03	23.75	300	Direct	100/130	7.5:1
L/TSIO-360-E*,EB	6		200-2575	4.44 x 3.87	360	*56.58	31.30	26.44	352*	Direct	100/130	7.5:1
TSIO-360-F*,FB	6		200-2575	4.44 x 3.87	360	*56.58	31.30	26.44	359*	Direct	100/130	7.5:1
TSIO-360-G*,GB	6		210-2700	4.44 x 3.87	360	*33.57	33.88	31.90	336*	Direct	100/130	7.5:1
TSIO-360-H*,HB	6		210-2800	4.44 x 3.87	360	35.34	31.38	22.43	313	Direct	100/130	7.5:1
0-470-G*	6		240-2600	5 x 4	470	37.56	33.58	26.69	431	Direct	91/96	8.0:1
0-470-J*	6		225-2550	5 x 4	470	36.03	33.32	27.75	380	Direct	80/87	7.0:1
0-470-K* & L*	6		230-2600	5 x 4	470	36.03	33.56	27.75	404	Direct	80/87	7.0:1
0-470-M*	6		240-2600	5 x 4	470	43.31	33.56	19.62	409	Direct	91/96	8.0:1
0-470-R	6		230-2600	5 x 4	470	36.03	33.56	28.42	401	Direct	80/87	7.0:1
0-470-S	6		230-2600	5 x 4	470	36.03	33.56	28.42	412	Direct	100/130	7.0:1
0-470-U	6		230-2400	5 x 4	470	36.03	33.56	28.42	412	Direct	100/130	8.6:1
IO-470-C*	6		250-2600	5 x 4	470	37.93	33.58	26.81	431	Direct	91/96	8.0:1
IO-470-D* & E*	6		260-2625	5 x 4	470	43.31	33.56	19.75	426	Direct	100/130	8.6:1
IO-470-F*	6		260-2625	5 x 4	470	37.22	33.56	23.79	426	Direct	100/130	8.6:1
IO-470-H*	6		260-2625	5 x 4	470	38.14	33.58	26.81	431	Direct	100/130	8.6:1
IO-470-J* & K*	6		225-2600	5 x 4	470	38.14	33.39	26.81	401	Direct	80/87	7.0:1
IO-470-L	6		260-2625	5 x 4	470	43.17	33.56	19.75	430	Direct	100/130	8.6:1
IO-470-M*	6		260-2625	5 x 4	470	47.16	33.56	19.75	430	Direct	100/130	8.6:1
IO-470-N	6		260-2625	5 x 4	470	38.14	33.58	26.81	433	Direct	100/130	8.6:1
IO-470-S*	6		260-2625	5 x 4	470	41.41	33.56	19.75	426	Direct	100/130	8.6:1
IO-470-U*	6		260-2625	5 x 4	470	44.14	33.86	19.75	423	Direct	100/130	8.6:1
IO-470-V*,VO	6		260-2625	5 x 4	470	43.69	33.56	19.75	423	Direct	100/130	8.6:1
TSIO-470-B*,C* & D*	6		260-2600	5 x 4	470	39.52	33.56	20.25	423	Direct	100/130	7.5:1
IO-520-A* & J	6		285-2700	5.25 x 4	520	41.41	33.56	19.75	431	Direct	100/130	8.5:1
IO-520-B*,BA*,BB	6		285-2700	5.25 x 4	520	39.71	33.58	26.71	422	Direct	100/130	8.5:1
IO-520-C*,CB	6		285-2700	5.25 x 4	520	42.88	33.56	19.75	415	Direct	100/130	8.5:1
IO-520-D	6	300@2850	285-2700	5.25 x 4	520	37.36	35.46	23.79	430	Direct	100/130	8.5:1
IO-520-E	6	300@2850	285-2700	5.25 x 4	520	47.66	33.56	19.75	427	Direct	100/130	8.5:1
IO-520-F	6	300@2850	285-2700	5.25 x 4	520	41.41	35.91	19.75	430	Direct	100/130	8.5:1
IO-520-K	6	300@2850	285-2700	5.25 x 4	520	40.91	33.56	19.75	428	Direct	100/130	8.5:1
IO-520-L	6	300@2850	285-2700	5.25 x 4	520	40.91	33.56	23.25	431	Direct	100/130	8.5:1
IO-520-M*,MB	6		285-2700	5.25 x 4	520	46.80	33.56	20.41	413	Direct	100/130	8.5:1
TSIO-520-B*,BB	6		285-2700	5.25 x 4	520	39.75	33.56	20.32	423	Direct	100/130	7.5:1
TSIO-520-C & H	6		285-2700	5.25 x 4	520	40.91	33.56	20.04	433	Direct	100/130	7.5:1
TSIO-520-D*,DB	6		285-2700	5.25 x 4	520	43.25	33.58	22.34	423	Direct	100/130	7.5:1
TSIO-520-E*,EB	6		300-2700	5.25 x 4	520	39.75	33.56	20.32	421	Direct	100/130	7.5:1
TSIO-520-G	6	300@2700	285-2600	5.25 x 4	520	40.91	33.56	20.04	433	Direct	100/130	7.5:1
TSIO-520-J*,JB,N*,NB	6		310-2700	5.25 x 4	520	54.36	33.56	22.50	412	Direct	100/130	7.5:1
TSIO-520-K,KB	6		285-2700	5.25 x 4	520	54.36	33.56	20.32	412	Direct	100/130	7.5:1
TSIO-520-L*,LB	6		310-2700	5.25 x 4	520	50.62	33.56	20.02	514*	Direct	100/130	7.5:1
TSIO-520-M & P	6	310@2700	285-2600	5.25 x 4	520	40.91	33.56	20.04	436	Direct	100/130	7.5:1
TSIO-520-R	6	310@2700	285-2600	5.25 x 4	520	40.91	33.56	23.54	436	Direct	100/130	7.5:1
TSIO-520-T	6		310-2700	5.25 x 4	520	*38.20	33.56	32.26	426*	Direct	100/130	7.5:1
TSIO-520-U*,UB	6		300-2700	5.25 x 4	520	*44.73	33.56	28.86	536*	Direct	100/130	7.5:1
TSIO-520-V*,VB	6		325-2700	5.25 x 4	520	39.25	33.56	20.41	456	Direct	100/130	7.5:1
TSIO-520-W*,WB	6		325-2700	5.25 x 4	520	*50.62	33.56	20.02	539*	Direct	100/130	7.5:1
GTSIO-520-C*	6		340-3200	5.25 x 4	520	42.56	34.04	23.10	481	Geared	100/130	7.5:1
GTSIO-520-D & H	6		375-3400	5.25 x 4	520	42.56	34.04	26.78	508	Geared	100/130	7.5:1
GTSIO-520-K	6		435-3400	5.25 x 4	520	*56.25	34.04	26.18	600*	Geared	100/130	7.5:1
GTSIO-520-L*	6		375-3350	5.25 x 4	520	43.87	34.04	26.41	502	Geared	100/130	7.5:1
GTSIO-520-M	6		375-3350	5.25 x 4	520	43.87	34.04	26.80	507	Geared	100/130	7.5:1
Tiara 6-285*	6		285-4000	4.88 x 3.62	406	40.11	32.91	24.22	382	Geared	100/130	9.0:1

† Includes IO-360-AB,CB,DB,GB,HB   * Rebuilt Only
* Includes Turbo and exhaust system

SOURCE: Teledyne Continental

TABLE 8-2 Continental Engines Versus Aircraft Installations

ENGINE	HP/RPM	AIRCRAFT	ENGINE	HP/RPM	AIRCRAFT
A-65	65/2300	AERONCA			CHAMPION CITABIA
		AIRCOUPE 415C			CHAMPION LANCER
		LUSCOMBE SILVAIRE 8F			SKY SCOOTER 211
		MOONEY CADET			STITS SA-3A
		PIPER CUB			TAYLORCRAFT F19
		TAYLOR J.T.1			ANDRESSON BA. 4B
		WASSMER JODEL D-112			AVIAMILAND P. 19
A-75	75/2600	STINSON			BEAGLE B 121 PUP 100
		PIPER			BOLKOW JUNIOR
		LUSCOMBE			CENTRE EST DR. 220 2+2
C-75	75/2275	ENGR. & RESEARCH			CENTRE EST-SIGILE RECORD
A-80	80/2700	STINSON			FAIRTRAVEL LINNET
C-85	85/2575	AERONCA			FOURNIER RF6
		ALON AIRCOUPE			MALMO MF.I.98 MILI-TRAINER
		CESSNA 140A			MALMO JUNIOR
		CULVER CADET			MS 880B RALLYE GLVB 100
		FUNK			PARTENANIA
		MIDGET MUSTANG MM 1-85			REIMS (CESSNA) FA-150
		STITS SA-3A			REIMS (CESSNA) F-105
		STITS SA-7D			ROLLASON-DRVINE CONDOR
		TURNER T-40			SAN JODEL D-150 MASCARET
		DURINE TURBULENT CP 304			SCINTEX SUPER EMERAUDE
		JURCA TEMPETE C			VICTA AIRTROURER
		TAYLOR J.T.2			WASSMER WA80 PIRANHA
		WASSMER JODEL D-11	0-200-B	100/2750	VOLMER VJ-22
C90-8F	95/2625	AERONCA C-3	0-240-A	130/2800	AERO ENGINE SERVICES
		PIPER PA-18 "95"			AIRTOURER T3
		BIANCO MACCHI MB308			FRA 150
		HINDUSTAN PUSHPAK HUL-26			MALMO MF1-9B
C90-12F	95/2625	ALON AIRCOUPE			ROLLASON CONDOR
		CESSNA 140A			HR200/100-AVIONS PIERRE ROBIN
		LUSCOMBE SILVAIRE 8F	0-240-E	130/2800	PRACTICA SPRITE
		PIPER PA-18 "95"			REIMS (CESSNA) FRA150
		A1SA-1-11B	0-300-A	145/2700	CESSNA 170B
C90-14F	95/2625	CESSNA 140A			CESSNA 172 SKYHAWK
		AERO DIFUSION JODEL D-1190S			MAULE JETSEN M-4
		MS RALLYE 880A			GOMHOURIA MK6
		SCINTEX EMERAUDE	0-300-C	145/2700	CESSNA 172A THRU E
		WASSMER JODEL D-120			& G SKYHAWK
C90-16F	95/2625	ALON AIRCOUPE			MS 885 SUPER RALLYE
		CESSNA 140A	0-300-D	145/2700	CESSNA 172B THRU E
		HELTON LARK 95			& G SKYHAWK
		AERO DIFUSION JODEL D1190-S			CESSNA 175B SKYHAWK
		MS RALLYE 880A			REIMS (CESSNA) F172
		SCINTEX EMERAUDE			*T-41A (CESSNA) USAF
		WASSMER JODEL D-120			CIERVA GRASSHOPPER
C125	125/2550	GLOBE SWIFT	GO-300-A	175/3200	CESSNA 175 SKYLARK
C145-2	145/2700	CESSNA 170	GO-300-C	175/3200	CESSNA 175A SKYLARK
		CESSNA 170A			CESSNA 175B SKYLARK
		CESSNA 170B	GO-300-E	175/3200	CESSNA 175C SKYLARK
E-165-2	165/2050	LUSCOMBE AIRTRAVELER			CESSNA P172D SKYHAWK
E-185-3	205/2600	NAVION	IO-346-A	165/2700	BEECH MUSKETEER CUSTOM III
E-185-8	205/2600	BEECH BONANZA A35			GADFLY E.S.102
E-185-9	205/2600	NAVION			PIEL EMERAUDE CP30
E-185-11	205/2600	BEECH BONANZA B35			PIEL EMERAUDE CP70
E-225-4	225/2650	NAVION			POULET
E-225-8	225/2650	BEECH BONANZA E35			STAMPE ET RENARD SV-4D
		BEECH BONANZA G35	IO-360-A	210/2800	CESSNA 336 SKYMASTER
0-200-A	100/2750	CESSNA 150 A THRU F			MAULE M-4 ROCKET
		CESSNA AEROBAT			BEAGLE B242C

TABLE 8-2 *(continued)*

ENGINE	HP/RPM	AIRCRAFT	ENGINE	HP/RPM	AIRCRAFT
IO-360-C/CB	210/2800	CESSNA 337 CESSNA 337A SUPER SKYMASTER *AERO BOERO 210* *REIMS (CESSNA) F-337* *O-2A (CESSNA 337) USAF* *O-2B (CESSNA 337) USAF*	0-470-S	230/2600	CESSNA 180 SKYWAGON CESSNA 182 SKYLANE CESSNA AG PICKUP *REIMS (CESSNA) F182*
IO-360-D/DB	210/2800	CESSNA 337 SKYMASTER CESSNA 337A SUPER SKYMASTER *BURNS BA-42* *AVIONS PIERRE ROBIN HR100/210* *AIRCRUISER* *AERO DIFUSION JODEL D 1190-S* *CIERVA GRASSHOPPER* *REIMS (CESSNA) FR172 ROCKET* *REGENTA L-42* *T41B (CESSNA 172) ARMY* *T41C (CESSNA 172) USAF* *O-2A (CESSNA 337) USAF* *O-2B (CESSNA 337) USAF*	0-470-U	230/2400	CESSNA 180 SKYWAGON CESSNA 182 SKYLANE CESSNA AG PICKUP *REIMS (CESSNA) F182*
			0-470-2	265/2600	*O-IC (CESSNA) ARMY*
			0-470-4	225/2600	*T-34 (MENTOR) NAVY*
			0-470-7	205/2600	*L-17 (NAVION) ARMY*
			0-470-11	213/2600	*L-19 (CESSNA) ARMY* *O-1 (CESSNA) ARMY*
			0-470-13A	225/2600	*PZL-104 WILGA-CP* *T-34 (MENTOR) USAF*
			0-470-15	213/2600	*L-19 (CESSNA) ARMY* *TO-1D (CESSNA) ARMY*
IO-360-G-GB	210/2800	CESSNA 337 SUPER SKYMASTER	IO-470-C	250/2600	BEECH BONANZA J35 BEECH BONANZA K35 BEECH BONANZA M35
IO-360-H-HB	210/2800	CESSNA 337 SUPER SKYMASTER *REIMS (CESSNA) F337*	IO-470-D	260/2625	AERO COMMANDER 200D BELLANCA 260A
IO-360-J-JB	210/2800	*REIMS (CESSNA) FR172*			CESSNA 310 C THRU H
IO-360-K-KB	195/2600	CESSNA 172 HAWK XP *REIMS (CESSNA) FR172 HAWK XP*			MEYERS 200 *BEAGLE A.O.P. MK11*
TSIO-360-A	210/2800	CESSNA SUPER SKYMASTER T337 *REIMS (CESSNA) FT337*			*FLETCHER FU-24* *FLETCHER FU-24A*
TSIO-360-B	210/2800	CESSNA SUPER SKYMASTER T337			*U-3B (CESSNA 310) USAF*
TSIO-360-C-CB	225/2800	CESSNA PRESSURIZED SUPER SKYMASTER *REIMS (CESSNA) FR337P*	IO-470-E	260/2625	CESSNA 210 CESSNA 210A CENTURION *PROCAER PICCHIO F15C*
LTSIO-360E-EB	200/2575	PIPER SENECA II *EMBRAER-810-SENECA II*	IO-470-F	260/2625	BELLANCA 260C CESSNA 185A THRU E SKYWAGON *U-17 (CESSNA 185) USAF*
TSIO-360F-FB	200/2575	PIPER-28RT-20IT TURBO ARROW IV	IO-470-G	260/2625	*YEOMAN CROPMASTER*
TSIO-360-FB	200/2575	PIPER-28-20IT-TURBO DAKOTA	IO-470-H	260/2625	NAVION RANGEMASTER G-1
TSIO-360G-GB	210/2700	MOONEY-M20K 231	IO-470-J	225/2600	BEECH DEBONAIR C33
TSIO-360H-HB	210/2800	CESSNA T337 TURBO SKYMASTER	IO-470-K	225/2600	BEECH DEBONAIR C33 BEECH BONANZA F33
0-470-A	225/2600	CESSNA 180 SKYWAGON	IO-470-L	260/2625	BEECH BARON B55 *T-42 (BEECH BARON) ARMY*
0-470-B	225/2600	CESSNA 310	IO-470-M	260/2625	AERO COMMANDER 500A
0-470-G	240/2600	BEECH BONANZA H35	IO-470-N	260/2625	BEECH BONANZA NP35 BEECH BONANZA G33
0-470-J	225/2550	CESSNA 180 SKYWAGON *HINDUSTAN HAOP-27 KRISSHAK*	IO-470-P	250/2600	*S1A1-MARCHETTI RIVIERA*
0-470-K	230/2600	BELLANCA CESSNA 180A CESSNA 180B	IO-470-R	250/2600	*AERMACCHI AL60* *YEOMAN CROPMASTER - 250R*
0-470-L	230/2600	CESSNA 180C THRU H SKYWAGON CESSNA 182A THRU G SKYLANE *PZL WILGA*	IO-470-S	260/2600	CESSNA 205A CESSNA 205B CESSNA 205G
0-470-M	240/2600	CESSNA 310A CESSNA 310B *U-3A (CESSNA 310) USAF*	IO-470-U	260/2625	CESSNA 210 CENTURION CESSNA 310 CESSNA 310J CESSNA 310J-1
0-470-P	240/2600	NAVION (CONVERSION)			CESSNA E310J
0-470-R	230/2600	CESSNA 180C THRU H SKYWAGON CESSNA 182 E. F. G. H. J SKYLANE CESSNA AG PICKUP WREN 460 *REIMS (CESSNA) F182*	IO-470-V	260/2625	CESSNA 310K CESSNA 310L CESSNA 310P CESSNA 310Q *HINDUSTAN H-APO-27 KRISHAK*

TABLE 8-2 *(continued)*

ENGINE	HP/RPM	AIRCRAFT	ENGINE	HP/RPM	AIRCRAFT
GIO-470-A	310/3200	*BEAGLE B20 BASSET*			BEECH BARON
		FLETCHER FU24A (OPTIONAL)			(COLEMILL CONVERSION)
TSIO-470-B	260/2600	CESSNA 320 SKYNIGHT			*PRINAIR DE HAVILLAND HERON*
		CESSNA 320A SKYNIGHT	IO-520-F	300/2850	CESSNA U206 STATIONAIR 6
		CESSNA 320A-1 SKYNIGHT			CESSNA 207 STATIONAIR 7
		AERMACCI-LOCKHEED AC-60B2			CESSNA STATIONAIR
		AERMACCI-LOCKHEED LASA			*AMBROSINI MF-15*
					FLETCHER FU-24A
TSIO-470-C	260/2600	CESSNA 320B SKYNIGHT			*PROCAER F-150 PICCHIO*
TSIO-470-D	260/2600	CESSNA 320C SKYNIGHT	IO-520-J	285/2700	CESSNA 210 CENTURION
IO-520-A	285/2700	AERO COMMANDER 200D	IO-520-K	300/2850	BELLANCA VIKING 300
		CESSNA 206 STATIONAIR			*AISI F.20 PEGASO*
		CESSNA U206A	IO-520-L	300/2850	CESSNA 210 CENTURION
		CESSNA P206A			CESSNA 210 CENTURION II
		CESSNA P206B	IO-520-M-MB	285/2700	CESSNA 310
		CESSNA 210D CENTURION	TSIO-520-B-BB	285/2700	CESSNA T310
		CESSNA 210E CENTURION			CESSNA 320D. E. F. SKYNIGHT
		CESSNA 210F CENTURION	TSIO-520-C	285/2700	CESSNA T206 (STATIONAIR)
		BELLANCA VIKING 300			CESSNA T210F-G CENTURION
		FLETCHER FU-24A			CESSNA SUPER SKYLANE
		YEOMAN CROPMASTER 285	TSIO-520D, DB	285/2700	BEECH BONANZA ST35
		TRANSAVIA AIRTRUCK			BEECH BONANZA V35A-TC
IO-520B	285/2700	BEECH BONANZA S35	TSIO-520E, EB	300/2850	CESSNA 401A, 401E, 402A, 402B
		BEECH BONANZA F33A	TSIO-520-G	300/2700	CESSNA T207 SKYWAGON
		BEECH BONANZA A36	TSIO-520-H	285/2700	CESSNA T206 STATIONAIR
		BEECH BONANZA V35B			CESSNA T210 CENTURION II
		BEECH BONANZA E33B	TSIO-520J, JB	310/2700	CESSNA 414
		BEECH BONANZA E33C	TSIO-520K, KB	285/2700	CESSNA 340
		BEECH BONANZA E33A	TSIO-520L, LB	310/2700	BEECH BARON 58TC, 58P
		BEECH BONANZA 36	TSIO-520-M	310/2700	CESSNA T206 STATIONAIR
		BEECH BONANZA C33A			CESSNA T207 SKYWAGON
		JANOX JAVILON	TSIO-520N, NB	310/2700	CESSNA 340
		NAVION MODEL H			CESSNA 414
IO-520-BA	285/2700	BEECH BONANZA F33A			CESSNA CHANCELLOR
		BEECH BONANZA V35B	TSIO-520-P	310/2700	CESSNA P210 CENTURION
IO-520-BB	285/2700	BEECH BONANZA V35B	TSIO-520-R	310/2700	CESSNA T210 CENTURION
		BEECH BONANZA A36	TSIO-520-T	310/2700	CESSNA T188 AG HUSKY
		BEECH BONANZA F33	TSIO-520U, UB	300/2700	BEECH BONANZA A36TC
		BEECH BONANZA F33A	TSIO-520V, VB	325/2700	CESSNA 402C
IO-520-C-CB	285/2700	BEECH BARON C55	TSIO-520W, WB	325/2700	BEECH BARON 58TC
		BEECH BARON D55			BEECH BARON 58P
		BEECH BARON E55	GTSIO-520-C	340/3200	CESSNA 411
		BEECH BARON 58			*AERMACCHI AM-3*
		WINDECKER EAGLE			*BEAGLE B 206S*
IO-520-D	300/2850	BELLANCA VIKING 300	GTSIO-520-D	375/3400	CESSNA 421A
		CESSNA A185E SKYWAGON	GTSIO-520-F	435/3400	AERO COMMANDER 685
		CESSNA AG WAGON B300	GTSIO-520-G	375/3400	*OV-22B (BEECH) USAF
		CESSNA 188 AG WAGON	GTSIO-520-H	375/3400	CESSNA 421A
		OMNIPAL CMELAK			CESSNA 421B (PRESS.)
		TRANSAVIA AIRTRUK	GTSIO-520-K	435/3400	AERO COMMANDER 685
		*U-17 (CESSNA 185) USAF	GTSIO-520-L	375/3400	CESSNA 421C GOLDEN EAGLE
IO-520-E	300/2850	AERO COMMANDER 500A	GTSIO-520-M	375/3400	CESSNA 404 TITAN
		(COLEMILL CONVERSION)	TIARA 6-285-C	285/4000	PIPER BRAVE
		CESSNA 310			*AVIONS PIERRE ROBIN HR 100/285*
		(COLEMILL CONVERSION)	W 670-23	240/2200	CESSNA 190
					MISC.

SOURCE: Teledyne Continental

TABLE 8-3 Lycoming Engines

FIXED WING AIRCRAFT ENGINES

MODEL	NO. CYLINDERS, BORE & STROKE	COMPRESSION RATIO	HP	RPM
O-235-C	4-4⅜x3⅞	6.75:1	108/115	2600/2800
O-235-L	4-4⅜x3⅞	8.50:1	105/112/118	2400/2600/2800
O-320-A, E	4-5⅛x3⅞	7.00:1	140/150	2450/2700
AEIO-320-E	4-5⅛x3⅞	7.00:1	150	2700
O-320-B, D	4-5⅛x3⅞	8.50:1	160	2700
O-320-H	4-5⅛x3⅞	9.00:1	160	2700
IO-320-B, C	4-5⅛x3⅞	8.50:1	160	2700
LIO-320-B, C	4-5⅛x3⅞	8.50:1	160	2700
O-360-A	4-5⅛x4⅜	8.50:1	180	2700
IO-360-B	4-5⅛x4⅜	8.50:1	180	2700
AEIO-360-A	4-5⅛x4⅜	8.70:1	200	2700
AEIO-360-B	4-5⅛x4⅜	8.50:1	180	2700
IO-360-A, C	4-5⅛x4⅜	8.70:1	200	2700
LIO-360-C	4-5⅛x4⅜	8.70:1	200	2700
TO-360-C	4-5⅛x4⅜	7.30:1	210	2575
GO-480-B	6-5⅛x3⅞	7.30:1	270*	3400
GO-480-C, G	6-5⅛x3⅞	8.70:1	295*	3400
IGSO-480-A, B (2)	6-5⅛x3⅞	7.30:1	340*	3400
O-540-B	6-5⅛x4⅜	7.20:1	235	2575
O-540-J	6-5⅛x4⅜	8.50:1	235	2400
O-540-A	6-5⅛x4⅜	8.50:1	250	2575
O-540-E	6-5⅛x4⅜	8.50:1	260	2700
IO-540-C	6-5⅛x4⅜	8.50:1	250	2575
IO-540-D	6-5⅛x4⅜	8.50:1	260	2700
AEIO-540-D	6-5⅛x4⅜	8.50:1	260	2700
IO-540-A, B, E	6-5⅛x4⅜	8.70:1	290	2575
IO-540-K	6-5⅛x4⅜	8.70:1	300	2700
IO-540-U	6-5⅛x4⅜	8.70:1	300	2700
TIO-540-A	6-5⅛x4⅜	7.30:1	310	2575
TIO-540-C	6-5⅛x4⅜	7.20:1	250	2575
TIO-540-F	6-5⅛x4⅜	7.30:1	325	2575
TIO-540-R	6-5⅛x4⅜	7.30:1	340	2575
TIO-540-J	6-5⅛x4⅜	7.30:1	350	2575
TIO-541-A	6-5⅛x4⅜	7.30:1	310	2575
TIO-541-E	6-5⅛x4⅜	7.30:1	380	2900
TIGO-541-E	6-5⅛x4⅜	7.30:1	425	3200
TIGO-541-D, G	6-5⅛x4⅜	7.30:1	450	3200
IGO-540-B (2)	6-5⅛x4⅜	8.70:1	350*	3400
IGSO-540-A, B (2)	6-5⅛x4⅜	7.30:1	380*	3400
IO-720-A, B	8-5⅛x4⅜	8.70:1	400	2650

MODEL DESIGNATION

I: Fuel Injection
G: Geared
S: Supercharged
O: Opposed Cylinder Arrangement
T: Turbocharged
L: Left Hand Rotation   AE: Aerobatic Engine

"Numbers" following letters indicate displacement in cubic inches

* 5 Min. T. O. Rating

(2) Dry Sump Engine

TABLE 8-3 *(continued)*

FUEL	HEIGHT	WIDTH	LENGTH	WEIGHT
80/87	22.40	32.00	29.56	213
100	22.40	32.00	29.05	218
80/87	22.99	32.24	29.56	244
80/87	23.18	32.24	29.05	258
100	22.99	32.24	29.56	255
100	24.46	32.68	32.26	253
100	19.22	32.24	33.59	259
100	19.22	32.24	33.59	259
100	24.59	33.37	29.56	265
100	24.84	33.37	29.81	270
100	19.35	34.25	29.81	299
100	24.84	33.37	29.81	275
100	19.35	34.25	29.81	293
100	19.48	34.25	33.65	306
100	21.02	36.25	34.50	343
80/87	28.02	33.12	38.64	432
100	28.02	33.12	38.64	444
100	22.81	33.12	47.56	513
80/87	24.56	33.37	37.22	372
100	24.56	33.37	38.93	356
100	24.56	33.37	38.42	375
100	24.56	33.37	37.22	375
100	24.46	33.37	38.42	375
100	24.46	33.37	39.34	381
100	24.46	33.37	39.34	384
100	19.60	34.25	39.34	412
100	19.60	34.25	38.93	438
100	21.00	34.25	38.93	422
100	22.71	34.25	51.34	511
100	30.33	33.37	40.38	456
100	22.42	34.25	51.34	514
100	22.60	34.25	51.52	521
100	22.56	34.25	51.50	518
100	21.38	34.25	49.09	549
100	25.17	35.66	50.70	596
100	22.65	34.86	57.57	706
100	22.65	34.86	57.57	706
100	21.66	34.25	46.38	500
100	20.30	34.25	56.74	541
100	22.53	34.25	46.08	568

SOURCE: Avco Lycoming

TABLE 8-4 Lycoming Engines Versus Aircraft Installations

	Direct-Drive Engine	
Engine model	Aircraft application	Hp rating
O-235-C1, -C1B	Piper, Call Air, Victa, Champion	115
O-235-C2A, -C2C, -E2A	Grumman American, Aero Boero 115	115
O-235-F2A, -F2B	S.O.C.A.T.A.	125
O-235-H2C	Robin	100
O-235-K2B, -L2B	Robin	118
O-290-D, -D2, -D2B, -D2C	Piper, Champion, Call Air	130/140
O-320-A2A, -A2B, -A2C	Piper, Call Air, Champion, Mooney, Colonial, Rawdon, Doyn, G.E.M.S., Aero 100	150
O-320-A2B (fuel pump & prov. for vac. pump)	Piper Cherokee, Bede	150
O-320-A3A, -A3B, -A3C	Piper, Mooney, Lake, Dinfia, Aviamilano	150
O-320-B2B, -B2C	Piper, Beagle, Aero Boero Urapula	160
O-320-B2B, -B2C (fuel pump & prov. for vac. pump)	Piper Cherokee	160
O-320-B3, -B3C, -D1A	Piper, Aerospace	160
O-320-D2A	Piper Cherokee	160
O-320-D2A (with gen. on remfg. only)	Robin, Fuji	160
O-320-D2B, -D2C	Beech, Beagle	160
O-320-D1F	Wassmer	160
O-320-E1A	Sud	150
O-320-E2A, -E2B (less gen.)	Piper	140/150
O-320-E2A (with gen. on remfg. only)	Seems, G.E.M.S., S.O.C.A.T.A.	150
O-320-E2C, -E2G, -E3D	Beech, Piper, Wassmer Grumman American	150
AIO-320-A, -B, -C	M.B.B. Monsun	160
IO-320-B1A	Piper	160
IO-320-C1A (for exh. turbo)	Piper	160
IO-320-D1A	M.B.B.	160
IO-320-E1A, -E2A	Champion	150
LIO-320-B1A	Piper	160

TABLE 8-4 *(continued)*

	Direct-Drive Engine	
Engine model	Aircraft application	Hp rating
LIO-320-C1A	Piper	160
O-340-A1A	Temco, Doyn, Mooney	170
O-360-A1A, -A1D, -A1F, -C1A, -A2G, -C2A, -C2d (12V)	Piper, Mooney, Lake, Beech, Call Air, Bede, Wassmer, Doyn, Neiva, Dinfia, Partenavia, Aero Boero 180	180
O-360-A1A (24V)	Beech, Saab, Siai-Marchetti	180
LIO-360	Hurricane Fiberglass	180
O-360-A1LD	Wassmer	180
O-360-A2A, -A3A, -A4A (less gen.)	Piper Cherokee, Pitts	180
O-360-A3A	C.A.A.R.P., Robin, S.O.C.A.T.A.	180
O-360-A4G, -A4J	Beech	180
O-360-A2D	Mooney, McCulloch	180
O-360-A5AD	Fuji	180
HO-360-B1A, -B1B	Hughes	180
HIO-360-A1A	Hughes	180 to 3,900 ft. Alt
HIO-360-B1A (12V-24V)	Hughes	180
HIO-360-C1A, -C1B	Enstrom	205
HIO-360-D1A (12V-24V)	Hughes	190
AIO-360-A1A	Special Aerobatic	200
IO-360-A1A, -A2A, (12V-24V)	Siai-Marchetti, Mooney	200
IO-360-A1B	Lake, Beech	200
IO-360-A1B6	Beech, Scottish Air, Saab	200
IO-360-A1D, -A2B	Beech	200
IO-360-B1A (Simmonds)	Beech	180
IO-360-B1B, -B1D, -B4A (Bendix)	Beech, United Consultants, Pitts, Fuji	180
AEIO-360-B1G6	Great Lakes	180
IO-360-B1E	Piper	180
IO-360-C1B	S.O.C.A.T.A.	200
IO-360-C1C	Piper	200
IO-360-C1D6, -C1E6	Aero Commander, Piper	200
IO-360-C1F	Miller	200

TABLE 8-4 *(continued)*

	Direct-Drive Engine	
Engine model	Aircraft application	Hp rating
LIO-360-C1E6	Piper	200
TIO-360-A1B	Siai-Marchetti	200
O-540-A1A5, -A1B5, -A1C5, -A1D5	Piper, Helio	250
O-540-A1D, -A2B	Aero, Dornier, Helio	250
O-540-A3D5	Piper (Navy Aztec)	250
O-540-B1A5, -B1B5	Piper	235
O-540-B2B5, -B2C5 (12V-24V)	Piper, Imco, Aero	235
O-540-B4B5	Piper Cherokee	235
O-540-E4A5 (12V-24V)	Siai-Marchetti, Piper, Aviamilano	260
O-540-E4B/5	Piper Cherokee	260
O-540-E4C5 (24V)	Britten-Norman	260
O-540-G1A5, -G2A5	Piper	260
O-540-H1B5D, -H2B5D	Embracer	260
IO-540-A1A5, -B1A5, -B1C5, -E1A5, -E1B5, (24V)	Riley, Aero, Dornier, Doyn	290
IO-540-C1B5	Piper	250
IO-540-C1C5	Piper	250
IO-540-C2C	Helio	250
IO-540-C4B5 (12V-24V)	Piper Aztec "C" and "D"	250
IO-540-D4A5	Piper Comanche	260
IO-540-G1A5, -G1B5, -G1C5, -G1D5, -G1E5 (12V-24V)	Smith Aero Star, Doyn, Helio, Bellanca, Pilatus, Aero, Tehno Import	290
IO-540-J4A5 (for exh. turbo)	Piper Aztec	250
IO-540-K1A5	Piper Cherokee	300
IO-540-K1B5	Evangel-Air	300
IO-540-K1B5	Britten-Norman	300
IO-540-K1C5 (24V for exh.turbo)	Riley	290
IO-540-K1E5, -K1F5, -K1F5D	Bellanca, Smith Aero Star, Embracer	300
IO-540-M1A5	Piper	300
IO-540-N1A5	Piper	260
IO-540-P1A5, -S1A5 (prov. for turbo)	Smith Aero Star	290

TABLE 8-4 *(continued)*

Direct-Drive Engine		
Engine model	Aircraft application	Hp rating
IO-540-R1A5	Piper	260
TIO-540-A1A, -A1B, -A2A, -A2B (stainless steel turbo.)	Piper	310
TIO-540-A2C (stainless steel turbo.)	Piper	310
TIO-540-C1A (stainless steel turbo.)	Piper	250
TIO-540-J2BD	Piper	350
LTIO-540-J2BD	Piper	350
TIO-541-A1A	Mooney	310
TIO-541-E1A4, -E1C4 (with safety valve)	Beech	380
TIO-541-E1A4, -E1C4 (without safety valve)	Beech	380
TIO-541-E1B4, -E1D4 (with safety valve)	Beech	380
TIO-541-E1B4, -E1D4 (without safety valve)	Beech	380
IO-720-A1A, -A1B	Piper, Imco, Riley, Pays, Aerospace, Excalibur	400
IO-720-B1B	RPM Commander	400
IO-720-C1B	Hindustan	400

Geared Engine		
GO-435-C2B2, -C2B2-6, -C2E	Aero, Beech, Helio, Riley, Widgeon	260
GO-480,B, -B1A6, -B1C, -B1D, -F1A6, -F2A6, -F4A6	Aero, Beech, Helio, Widgeon, Dornier, Utva	270/175
GO-480-D1A	Aero	275
GO-480-G1A6, -G1D6, -G1H6, -G1J6, -G2D6, -G2F6	Beech, Helio, Widgeon, Utva	295
GO-480-G1B6	Aero	295
GSO-480-B1A6, -B1B3, -B1B6, -B1C5, -B1J6	Aero, Beech, Trecker, Dornier, Pilatus, C.Itoh, Utva, Piaggio	340
IGSO-480-A1A6, -A1B6	Beech	340
IGSO-480-A1C6, -A1F6	Fuji	340
IGSO-480-A1D6, -A1E6	Beech, Dornier	340

163

TABLE 8-4 (continued)

Engine model	Aircraft application	Hp rating
Direct-Drive Engine		
IGO-540-A1A, -A1C, -B1A, -B1C	Aero, Pilatus, Tehno Import, U.T.V.A.L	350
IGSO-540-A1A, -A1C	Beech, Piaggio	380
IGSO-540-A1D, -A1E	Beech, Dornier	380
IGSO-540-B1A	Aero, Excalibur	380
TIGO-541-E1A,-D1A (with safety valve)	Piper	425
TIGO-541-E1A, -D1A (without safety valve)	Piper	425
Vertical Engine		
VO-360-B1A	Brantley	180
IVO-360-A1A	Brantley	180
VO-435-A1D, -A1E (without inconel valves)	Bell, Agusta, Kawasaki	260
VO-435-A1D, -A1E (inconel valves)	Bell, Agusta	260
VO-435-A1F	Bell, Agusta, Kawasaki	260
VO-435-B1A (12V-24V)	Bell	265
TVO-435-A1A	Bell, Agusta, Kawasaki	260
TVO-435-B1A, -B1B	Bell, Agusta, Kawasaki, Westland-Ltd.	270
TVO-435-F1A	Bell	280
TVO-435-D1A, -D1B, -G1A	Bell, Agusta, Kawasaki, Westland Ltd.	270
VO-540-B1A, -B1C	Hiller	305
VO-540-B2A, -B2C	Hiller	305
VO-540-B1B3 (inconel valves)	Bell, Agusta	305
VO-540-B1D, -B1E, -B2D, -B2E	Hiller	305
VO-540-C1A, -C1B	Hiller	305 to 3,000 ft. Alt.
VO-540-C2A, -C2B	Hiller	305 to 3,000 ft. Alt.
IVO-540-A1A	Brantley	305 ft. 3,000 ft. Alt.
TIVP-540-A2A	Hiller	315 to 14,000 ft. Alt.

Source: Avco Lycoming.

TABLE 8-5 Recommended TBO (Certified Air-Cooled Aircraft Engines)

CONTINENTAL		LYCOMING	
Engine	TBO	Engine	TBO
A-65	1800 hours	0-235	2000 hours
C-85	1800 hours	0-290D-2	1500 hours
C-90	1800 hours	0-320	2000 hours
0-200A	1800 hours	0-360	2000 hours
0-300	1800 hours	IO-360 (180 hp)	2000 hours
G0-300	1200 hours	IO-360 (200 hp)	1600 hours
IO-360	1500 hours	TIO-360	1600 hours
TSIO-360	1400 hours	GO-435	1200 hours
IO-520	1500 hours	0-435	1200 hours
TSIO-520	1400 hours	GSO-480	1200 hours
GTSIO-520	1200 hours	IGSO-480	1200 hours
		0-540	2000 hours
		TIGO-540A	1800 hours
		IO-720	1800 hours

Time between overhaul (TBO) becomes increasingly important as labor rates continue to skyrocket along with production aircraft costs. The above table is included for comparison purposes because this item, too, is a factor to be considered in finally determining your powerplant installation.

UNCERTIFIED ENGINES

As the number and different types of homebuilt aircraft increase, so do the available engine conversions. These range from essentially lawn-mower or chain-saw air-cooled 2-cycle units through many Volkswagen (VW) modifications differing greatly in quality and dependability to very high-powered, liquid-cooled automobile engines.

Limbach of Sassenberg, Federal Republic of Germany, produces high-quality, single- and dual-ignition engines based upon the VW powerplant. However, these models are so modified and so expensive that for North American use a good used, certified Continental or Lycoming engine would be cheaper, more readily serviceable, and at least as reliable if not more so.

Since many VW powerplant components and complete conversions are regularly advertised in EAA's *Sport Aviation* magazine, this well-known type will not be further discussed here except to note that a heavy crankshaft version is really essential for a safe, reliable, and comparatively long life installation. Remember that production automobile engines are not intended to operate at nearly full power for their entire service life, although that is what aircraft installations require from any low-power engine.

To aid in powerplant selection, a few of the interesting homebuilt powerplants currently available will be briefly reviewed in sequence of increasing power. While this listing by no means includes all uncertified engines on the market, it will provide some idea of what engines other than VW modifications can be obtained for your airplane.

Soarmaster Power Pack

Striplin Aircraft Corporation, P.O. Box 2001, Lancaster, CA 93534 offers two engines, Models PP-106 SS single-cylinder and PP-106 ST 2-cylinder, complete power systems for ultralight aircraft. These air-cooled engines weigh 28 and 43 lbs, respectively, and are equipped with aluminum mufflers, rubber shock absorbers, racing-chain, propeller-drive reduction systems, and propellers. They have pull-cord starters and are conversions of 10-hp Chrysler engines.

Power Package Kits

Manufactured by Ultralight Flying Machines of Wisconsin, P.O. Box 248, Kansas-ville, WI 53139. John Moody, who developed one of the first powered conversions of a hang glider, has modified existing small, 2-cycle, air-cooled engines into three ultralight powerplants of the 12- to 20-hp class. These are:

McCulloch 101 direct-drive

Maximizer West Bend 820

Maximizer McCulloch 101

These power kits include shock mounts, belt reduction drive for the Maximizer units, mufflers, and all installation hardware.

Rotec Power Units

Rotec Engineering Inc., P.O. Box 124, Duncanville, TX 75116 offers ultralight, air-cooled, 11- and 12-hp powerplants with direct- or reduction-drive systems complete with a selection of propellers, ram tube intakes, aluminum mufflers, and shock mounts. Accessories include head temperature gauge, tachometer, and optional reed intake.

Chotia 460

This engine comes from Weedhopper of Utah, Inc., P.O. Box 2253, Ogden, UT 84404. John Chotia, well known to hang-glider and ultralight enthusiasts, has developed what is probably the most powerful small engine available to homebuilders at reasonable cost and weight. The single-cylinder, air-cooled Chotia 460 develops 25 hp at 31.50 lbs installed weight. This output makes the 460 worth considering as an

Figure 8-1 The Chotia 460 develops 25 hp at 31.50 lb. *(Weedhopper photo.)*

engine for powered sailplanes as well as ultralights. A typical Chotia 460 installation in the Weedhopper ultralight is shown in Figure 8-1 (see the design on page 137).

RotorWay RW-100

This comes from RotorWay Aircraft, Inc., 14805 South Interstate 10, Tempe, AZ 85284. B. J. Schramm, well known for his Scorpion homebuilt helicopter (see the design on page 108), has continued development of the RotorWay 4-cycle, water-cooled engine to include both normally aspirated (unblown, ambient combustion air intake) and turbosupercharged models. These engines are shock-mounted, gear-reduction drive designs having the specifications given in Table 8-6. The normally aspirated RW-100 performance characteristics are shown in Figure 8-2.

TABLE 8-6 Normally Aspirated Versus Turbosupercharged RW-100

	Normally aspirated	Turbosupercharged
Dry weight, lb	170	185
hp	100	120 @ 70% boost
Displacement, cu in	133	133
Cooling	Water	Water
Specific Fuel Consumption (SFC), lb/hp/hr	0.4	0.4
rpm	3500	3500

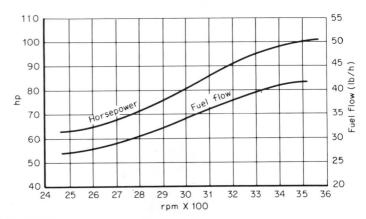

Figure 8-2 RW-100 performance characteristics.

Javelin Ford 140 T

Developed by Javelin Aircraft Company, Inc., 1978 Easy Street, Wichita, KS 67230. After 2 years of design and flight work, Dave Blanton (see Witchawk on page 63) has produced a liquid-cooled modification of a standard 140-cu-in, 4-cylinder Ford engine. Delivering 220 hp at 2700 propeller rpm, this turbosupercharged powerplant

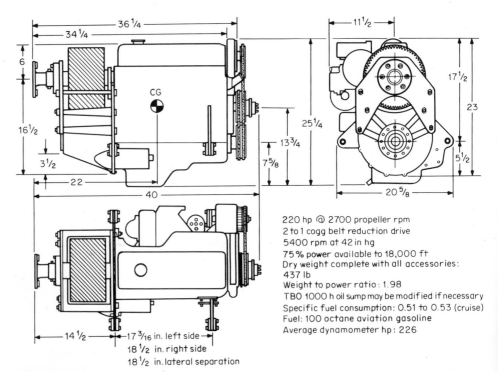

220 hp @ 2700 propeller rpm
2 to 1 cogg belt reduction drive
5400 rpm at 42 in hg
75% power available to 18,000 ft
Dry weight complete with all accessories:
437 lb
Weight to power ratio : 1.98
TBO 1000 h oil sump may be modified if necessary
Specific fuel consumption: 0.51 to 0.53 (cruise)
Fuel: 100 octane aviation gasoline
Average dynamometer hp: 226

Figure 8-3 The 220-hp Javelin Ford 140 T engine. *(Courtesy of Javelin Aircraft Company.)*

will deliver 75 percent power at 18,000 feet and weighs 437 lbs dry including all accessories and 2 to 1 belt-reduction drive. A conversion manual and all reduction-drive components are available from the factory. This engine has been extensively flight-tested in various aircraft and has the installation dimensions shown in Figure 8-3 as supplied by Javelin Aircraft.

Geschwender Engines

Available from Geschwender Aeromotive, 4131 Northwest 36 Street, Lincoln, NE 68524. For the past 12 years, Geschwender has been developing a line of liquid-cooled automotive conversion engines suitable for aircraft use. Ranging at the upper end of propeller-driven powerplant requirements, these engines are suitable for high-performance custom and racing aircraft and have also found increasing acceptance on agricultural aircraft (which are licensed to operate in the FAA Restricted Category). While not an engine for your Thorp 18 or RV-3, turbo models of these conversions might be fitted to the Brokaw Bullet or Sequoia 300 high-performance aircraft (see the designs on pages 54 and 83).

Typical specifications for these engines are given in Table 8-7, with additional models under development by Geschwender.

Other

If you are planning an antique or custom development requiring an upright in-line engine, B & F Aircraft Supply Inc., 6141 West 95 Street, Oak Lawn, IL 60453 converts inverted Ranger air-cooled engines into upright types delivering power similar

TABLE 8-7 Geschwender Liquid-Cooled Automotive Engine Conversion Specifications for Aircraft Application

Engine model	Dyno hp/rpm	Wgt. (lb)	L (in)	W (in)	H (in)	rpm prop/engine	Ratio	Fuel grade
ILCV351	330/5500	565	46.5	22	24	2860/5500	1.923-1	100–130
						2384/5500	2.307-1	
						2270/5500	2.423-1	
TILCV351 turbo	462/5500	600	49	25	29	2860/5500	1.923-1	100–130
						2384/5500	2.307-1	
						2270/5500	2.423-1	
ILCV460	430/5250	700	49	23.5	28	2730/5250	1.923-1	100–130
						2275/5250	2.307-1	
						2166/5250	2.423-1	
TILCV460 turbo	602/5250	750	52	26.5	31	2730/5250	1.923-1	100–130
						2275/5250	2.307-1	
						2166/5250	2.423-1	

to the original inverted models. The B & F 6-cylinder Model 444, for example, delivers 200 hp at 376 lbs. This compares favorably to a 1913 6-cylinder Daimler weight of 176 kg (388 lbs) for 100 hp and is the engine used in the Etrich Taube replica under construction for the Owls Head Museum at Rockland Airport.

Additional homebuilt powerplant information will be found in *Engines for Homebuilts* (see Ref. 8.2). In the final analysis, however, the best initial source for converted-engine performance and installation requirements will probably be members of one of your local EAA chapters; they have "been there" and know from experience just how the different conversions behave in their own aircraft. In view of this, be sure to review any "final" engine selection with someone who has installed the same type and flown behind it for some time; to do otherwise might be a source of future regret. Further information concerning powerplant installation and cooling will be found in *Design for Flying* (see Ref. 8.3), which thoroughly covers small-aircraft requirements.

REFERENCES

8.1 *General Aviation Engine Suspensions,* Technical Reference LB-571, Lord Kinematics, 1635 West 12 Street, Erie, PA 16512.

8.2 J. Christy, *Engines for Homebuilts,* Tab Books, Summit, PA 1977.

8.3 David B. Thurston, *Design for Flying,* McGraw-Hill, New York, 1978, chap. 11.

THREE

Materials
and
Methods

chapter NINE

Shop Requirements

It is quite obvious that a large airplane will require more assembly area than will a small one. What is not quite so obvious, however, soon becomes crystal-clear once construction gets under way: *Regardless of the size of the final airplane, it is essential that adequate working space be provided around all assembly fixtures and final assembly areas.* Since you will probably be working on a homebuilt airplane for a number of years, the inconvenience of cramped quarters can eventually discourage construction and may well be one of the major reasons for discontinued projects. The constant annoyance of banging elbows plus not having enough clearance for drilling and riveting or sufficient room to trial-fit parts into place probably adds 30 to 50 percent to the time necessary to complete construction.

Considering that one of the main reasons for beginning a homebuilt airplane is to enjoy a creative hobby, make sure you will be working in an area that will satisfy your particular requirements—and these requirements will vary from builder to builder. While some people can cruise for long periods in a 20-ft sailboat, others need a 30- to 40-footer to be comfortable. Regardless of your estimates or what the design literature may suggest, anything less than 5 ft of clearance all around jigs or assembly fixtures will eventually prove restrictive.

In addition, space is required for the basic working tools, such as a band saw, air compressor, table saw, drill press, belt and disc sander, special cutting tools, perhaps a welding cart, and so on. All the purchased hardware and equipment plus structural materials—sheet metal or wood, tubing, and similar items—must be stored, so racks and shelves are required at some remote but readily accessible portion of the shop. Ideally, all of the above should be located so they will not have to be moved about as work progresses. If you must set up a band saw or drill press each time it is to be used or disconnect and move machinery to reach the sheet-metal storage rack, working time and annoyance increase at an alarming rate. Although not always apparent, inadequate shop space or inconvenient layout is one contributing factor to the great difference in assembly time between builders of the same aircraft design.

To sum up this recommendation: if you have a fuselage that will be 4 ft wide by 20 ft long when assembled, an area of about 15 by 30 ft should be allocated to this structure alone. Of course, an additional 200-sq-ft minimum should be set aside for the standing power tools, another 100 sq ft for materials, templates, and parts storage, and sufficient space for a couple of workbenches plus detail-parts fabrication. Thus the basic, minimum homebuilt-aircraft assembly area for a two- to four-place airplane will total about 900 sq ft. And if you have a fuselage that will be only 3 ft wide by 15 ft long, the accompanying area reduction compared to the larger 4- by 20-ft fuselage will be only 40 sq ft (1-ft width by 20-ft length plus 4-ft width by 5-ft shorter fuselage equals 40-sq-ft area reduction). All of this is presented to demonstrate that required shop space is not directly proportional to the size of the airplane under construction. Plan for adequate shop area before fully digging into any project.

Many builders spend the first year on their airplanes putting additions onto their homes or constructing a separate assembly shop somewhere on their property. Others relocate their automobiles outside on their driveways for a few years while transforming their two-car garages into shop areas. Although a 25- by 30-ft garage might provide an initial working space, this area will be found less than ideal as the project progresses, while nature slowly destroys the car finish as time goes by.

I fully realize many aircraft have been assembled in garages, living rooms, and so on, but I still maintain that assembly time would have been reduced if a larger space had been available. As a useful compromise, a basement assembly area can be satisfactory if headroom permits and outside access is wide enough to allow for removal of assembled components.

Tony Bingelis, an active member of EAA and a regular contributor to *Sport Aviation,* has presented such thorough coverage of shop tools and practices in *The Sportplane Builder* (see Ref. 9.1) that this material need not be repeated here. The FAA manuals listed in Reference 9.2 are particularly helpful during the final phases of aircraft-equipment planning and installation. They also provide information about standard aircraft shop techniques and repair practices. The major items covered in these publications are radio and antenna installation; electrical systems; oxygen installation; shoulder-harness types and their installation; wooden-structure assembly, finish, and repair; welding practices; metal repair; fabric covering; control-cable specifications and assembly procedures; aircraft hardware; materials identification; landing-gear equipment; and snow-ski installation.

Builders constructing all-metal aircraft with radiused sheet trailing edges on the wings, flaps, and tail surfaces have difficulty forming the tight bends required without also wrinkling or otherwise damaging the skin itself. The simple fold brake shown in Figure 9-1 seems to do the job well and might be considered the next time such bends are required. Of course, the die thickness (and hinge offset) can be modified as necessary to provide the desired bend radius.

The search for tools and shop procedures consumes many hours during the start-up of any new shop project. This is especially true for homebuilders working on their first airplane. To ease the pain a bit, lists of tool sources (see Ref. 9.3), homebuilt publications (see Ref. 9.4), and books covering shop practice (see Ref. 9.5) have been

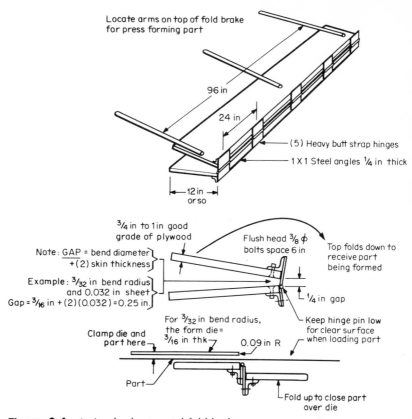

Locate arms on top of fold brake
for press forming part

96 in

24 in

(5) Heavy butt strap hinges

1 X 1 Steel angles ¼ in thick

12 in
or so

¾ in to 1in good
grade of plywood

Flush head ⅜ φ
bolts space 6 in

Top folds down to
receive part
being formed

Note: GAP = bend diameter
+(2) skin thickness

Example: ³⁄₃₂ in bend radius
and 0.032 in sheet
Gap = ³⁄₁₆ in + (2)(0.032) = 0.25 in.

¼ in gap

Keep hinge pin low
for clear surface
when loading part

For ³⁄₃₂ in bend radius,
the form die =
³⁄₁₆ in thk

0.09 in R

Clamp die and
part here

Part

Fold up to close part
over die

Figure 9-1 A simple sheet-metal fold brake.

included as useful references. I am indebted to Alfred P. Scott, president of Sequoia Aircraft, for some of this material, which was compiled for builders of his Sequoia, Kodiak, and Falco F.8L aircraft.

REFERENCES

9.1 Tony Bingelis, *The Sportplane Builder.* Order from Tony Bingelis, 8509 Greenflint Lane, Austin, TX 78759. Price: $14.95 postpaid.

9.2 FAA Advisory Circular, AC No. 43.13-1A, Change 1: *Acceptable Methods, Techniques and Practices—Aircraft Inspection and Repair,* May 12, 1975. Available from the Superintendent of Documents, U.S. Government Printing Office, Washington, DC 20402. Price: $3.70 in 1980. Order Stock No. 050-011-00058-5.
FAA Advisory Circular, AC No. 43.13-2A, *Acceptable Methods, Techniques and Practices—Aircraft Alteration,* June 9, 1977. Available from the Superintendent of Documents, U.S. Government Printing Office, Washington, DC 20402. Price: $2.75 in 1980. Order Stock No. 050-007-00407-9.

9.3 Aircraft Tools

Aircraft Tool Supply Company, 5738 F 41, Oscoda, MI 48750. Good source. Phone orders welcome, and bank cards accepted.

USATCO's Air World, 1136 Arlington Avenue, Franklin Square, NY 11010. Excellent source.

U.S. Industrial Tool and Supply, 13541 Auburn, Detroit, MI 48223. Excellent source of tools and riveting equipment.

Dale Williams Metal Fabricator, 2484 Pinto Lane, Norco, CA 91760. Source of tubing notchers, porto metal formers, bead rollers, and flame cutting pattern tracers.

General Tools

The L. S. Starret Company Catalogue, L. S. Starrett Company, Athol, MA. Suppliers of calipers, rulers, protractors, and other measuring tools.

The Shop Tool Manual, Brown & Sharp Manufacturing Company, Precision Park, North Kingstown, RI 02852.

Rockwell Professional Power Tool Catalogue
Rockwell Industrial Power Tool Catalogue
Available from local distributor.

Garrett Wade Company, 302 Fifth Avenue, New York, NY 10001. Supplies an excellent line of woodworking tools and books. Expensive, but they have superior merchandise and give excellent service.

Woodcraft Supply Corporation, 313 Montvale Avenue, Woburn, MA 01801. Supplier of woodworking tools and books giving excellent service.

JET Equipment & Tools, 1901 Jefferson Avenue, Tacoma, WA 98402. Carries a line of inexpensive lathes and milling machines.

Taps, Dies and Gages Catalogue
Cutting Tool Catalogue
Cleveland Twist Drill Company, P.O. Box 6656, Cleveland, OH 44101.
Available from local distributor.

9.4 Publications

Sport Aviation, P.O. Box 229, Hales Corners, WI 53130. You should join the EAA if you are not a member. The EAA is largely responsible for the freedom we enjoy in this country to build and fly our own aircraft and deserves support for that reason alone. *Sport Aviation,* the magazine of the EAA, contains a great deal of interest because it is entirely devoted to the subject of homebuilt aircraft.

Aviation Mechanics Journal, P.O. Box 750, Basin, WY 82410. This monthly magazine by the Aviation Maintenance Foundation is sold primarily to A&P mechanics. It is a professional publication worth subscribing to.

Homebuilt Aircraft, 606 Wilshire Boulevard, Santa Monica, CA 90406. This magazine by the editors of *Plane & Pilot* is devoted to the subject of amateur aircraft construction.

Trade-A-Plane, Crossville, TN 38555. This is the best way to buy or sell anything in aviation.

Aviation Mechanics Bulletin, Flight Safety Foundation, Inc., 5510 Columbia Pike, Arlington, VA 22204. Bimonthly magazine for A&P mechanics.

Fine Woodworking, The Taunton Press, 52 Church Hill Road, Box 355, Newtown, CT 06470. This superb magazine is devoted to "making beautiful things from wood." There is only an occasional article on aircraft construction, but each issue is crammed full of articles on wood-working techniques. You will also find tools advertised here that you will not see elsewhere.

Wood Working, Quailcraft, Pankridge Street, Crondall, Farnham, Surrey, *England.* English equivalent of *Fine Woodworking.* A superb publication devoted to the serious worker.

Hemmings Motor News, Box 380, Bennington, VT 05201. The *Trade-A-Plane* of antique automobiles. There isn't anything about aircraft in the publication, but it is a great source of information on suppliers of upholstery materials, leathers, and so on.

9.5 Aircraft Construction Books

> *Airframe & Powerplant Mechanics General Handbook*
> *Airframe & Powerplant Mechanics Powerplant Handbook*
> *Airframe & Powerplant Mechanics Airframe Handbook*
> By Department of Transportation, FAA. Reprinted by Aviation Maintenance Foundation, P.O. Box 739, Basin, WY 82410. These books are required reading if you are not an A&P.

> *Aircraft Hydraulic Systems*
> *Aircraft Instrument Systems*
> *Aircraft Oxygen Systems*
> *Aircraft Fuel Metering Systems*
> *Basic Electronics for A&P Mechanics*
> *Aircraft Ignition Systems*
> By Aviation Maintenance Foundation, P.O. Box 739, Basin, WY 82410. Good course in basic aircraft systems.

> *Standard Aircraft Handbook,* Leavell and Bungay. Available from Zenith Aviation Books, Route 2, Box 341, North Branch, MN 55056. An essential handbook. Required reading.

> *Sheet Metal Volume I*
> *Sheet Metal Volume II*
> Available from EAA, P.O. Box 229, Hales Corners, WI 53130. Excellent Air Force manuals reprinted by EAA. Required reading if you do not get *Airframe & Powerplant Mechanics Airframe Handbook,* which is more complete and covers everything that is in *Sheet Metal.*

> *Aircraft Drafting & Detail Design* (two volumes). Available from Zenith Aviation Books, Route 2, Box 341, North Branch, MN 55056. Excellent course. Required reading if you have trouble reading plans.

> *Light Airplane Construction for Amateur Builders*
> *Pazmany PL-4A Construction Manual*
> By Ladislao Pazmany. Available from Pazmany Aircraft Corporation, P.O. Box 80051, San Diego, CA 92138. Two excellent construction manuals. Helpful reading for the inexperienced builder.

> *Custom Built Sport Aircraft Handbook,* Available from EAA, P.O. Box 229, Hales Corners, WI 53130. A guide to dealing with FAA requirements and procedures.

Aircraft Painting and Finishing Manual, Randolph Products Company. Available from Randolph Products Company, P.O. Box 67, Carlstadt, NJ 07072, or Aviation Maintenance Foundation, P.O. Box 739, Basin, WY 82410. A useful reference for painting and surface preparation.

Modern Welding, Althouse, Turnquist, and Bowditch. Available from Zenith Aviation Books, Route 2, Box 341, North Branch, MN 55056.

The Use and Care of Twist Drills
The Use and Care of Reamers
The Use and Care of Taps
By Cleveland Twist Drill Company, P.O. Box 91276, Cleveland, OH 44101. Available from local distributors.

Power Tool Know How. Available from Sears Roebuck & Company. Good manual on use of band saws, planers, miter boxes, sharpening tools, table saws, wood lathes, and stationary sanders.

Basic Hand Tools, vols. I and II. Available from EAA, P.O. Box 229, Hales Corners, WI 53130. Good primers on hand tools.

Complete Metalworking Manual, R. H. Cooley. Available from Brookstone Company, 123 Vose Farm Road, Peterborough, NH 04358.

Wood Aircraft Inspection and Fabrication, ANC-19. Long-out-of-print government bulletin. This is the "Bible" of aircraft woodwork. Every wood builder will profit from reading it. Reproductions can be obtained from John Roby, 3703 Nassau Drive, San Diego, CA 92115.

Aircraft Spruce & Plywood, MIL-S-6073. The basic military specification for aircraft-grade wood, and builders might find it interesting. Those wood-airplane builders who live in areas where Sitka spruce is available may want to purchase and select their own spruce. This specification gives all the necessary information for grading the wood. Available from Aircraft Spruce and Specialty Company or John Roby, 3703 Nassau Drive, San Diego, CA 92115.

Adhesive Bonding of Wood, M. L. Selbo. Originally published by the Department of Agriculture as Technical Bulletin No. 1512, this excellent book covers the full range of glues for wood. While not specifically intended for aircraft work only, the book covers all of the glues used in aircraft work, and it is the best text available on the subject. The book is published by Sterling Publishers, Inc., 2 Park Avenue, New York, NY 10016.

Wood Bending Manual, W. C. Stevens and N. Turner. This book covers the subject well and much of it applies to aircraft work, even though the book is not specifically written with aircraft in mind. Available from Woodcraft Supply Corporation, 313 Montvale Avenue, Woburn, MA 01801.

CAM 18. *Maintenance, Repair and Alteration of Airframes, Powerplants, Propellers and Appliances,* FAA, 1959. This basic manual, out of print for some time, has been reprinted by the EAA. Available from the EAA, P.O. Box 229, Hales Corner, WI 53130.

Aircraft Woodwork, Ruth Spencer. A very good little book with many photos and construction techniques detailed. Available from Zenith Aviation Books, Route 2, Box 341, North Branch, MN 55056.

Materials, Processes, and Finishes

chapter TEN

MATERIALS

Finding suitable materials and necessary hardware sometimes seems to take as much time as the actual detail parts layout, fabrication, and assembly. Knowing just what to ask for and, equally important, where to ask for it can save many hours better spent in construction; and that is the purpose of this chapter.

Figure 10-1 provides specifications for the aluminum and steel alloys commonly used in aircraft structures. If you are building in wood, it is simply necessary to specify the type (Sitka spruce, birch plywood, maple, or whatever) called for on the detail drawings and to note that all items must be certified as aircraft quality material.

When using aluminum alloy extrusion, it is worth noting that 2014-T6 is usually less expensive than 2024-T4 (although still far from cheap), and is slightly stronger as well. I believe this is the only occasion in aircraft construction where something better or stronger is not proportionally more expensive; so take advantage of the opportunity when you can, especially for main beam cap strip angles and similar structural members.

Comparative material properties for the commonly used aluminum and steel alloys are given in Figure 10-2 for the benefit of builders who may wish to do some modification or original design work of their own. By comparison, 2014-T6 extrusion has an ultimate tensile stress value of at least 60,000 lb/sq in, indicating about 5 percent greater strength than extruded 2024-T4 at a slightly lower cost as noted above.

Whenever possible, all-metal, aluminum alloy aircraft should be built with alclad sheet parts and skins. Alclad material has a very thin layer of nearly pure aluminum physically roll-bonded to each side of the basic alloy core. Thus alclad 2024-T3 consists of a sheet of bare 2024-T3 with thin aluminum foil on each face. For a given total thickness, it is apparent that bare material will be stronger than alclad sheet of the same alloy because pure aluminum has less strength than aluminum alloy. As an example, .040 bare 2024-T3 will have greater tensile, shear, and bearing stress values than .040 alclad (or "clad") 2024-T3 because all .040 in of bare sheet consists of alloy material, which is stronger than pure aluminum. This relationship is shown by the comparative tensile stress values for 2024-T3 given in Figure 10-3. As would

ALUMINUM ALLOYS

Type	Bare sheet and plate	Clad sheet and plate	Rolled or drawn bars, rods, and wire	Drawn tubing	Extruded bars, rods, tubing, and shapes	Forgings	Castings
2014	H.T. to -T6 AMS 4029	QQ-A-250/3	QQ-A-225/4		QQ-A-200/2	MIL-A-22771 Type 2014	
2024	QQ-A-250/4	QQ-A-250/5	QQ-A-225/6	WW-T-700/3	QQ-A-200/3		
5052	QQ-A-250/8		QQ-A-225/7	WW-T-700/4			
6061	QQ-A-250/11		QQ-A-225/8	WW-T-700/6 Hydraulic tubing MIL-T-7081	QQ-A-200/8	MIL-A-22771 Type 6061	
6063					QQ-A-200/9		
7075	QQ-A-250/12	QQ-A-250/13	QQ-A-225/9	WW-T-700/7	QQ-A-200/11	MIL-A-22771 Type 7075	
356							QQ-A-601 Cond. T6
Tenzaloy							MIL-A-12033 Class 2

STEEL ALLOYS

Type	Sheet, strip, and plate	Condition	Maximum strength	Seamless tubing	Bars and forgings
1015–1025	Commercial	Mild steel	55,000 psi	MIL-T-5066	Commercial
4130	MIL-S-18729	Normalized / Heat treat	<.187 thick—95,000 / >.187 thick—90,000 / 150,000 psi max	MIL-T-6736	MIL-S-6758
4140		Heat treat	200,000 psi max	AMS 6381 AMS 6390	MIL-S-5626
4340	AMS 6359	Heat treat	260,000 psi max	AMS 6415	MIL-S-5000
321 & 347	MIL-S-6721	Stainless steel		MIL-T-8606	

Figure 10-1 Materials specifications for aluminum and steel alloys commonly used in aircraft construction.

Material →	2024-T3 Alclad sht.	2024-T4 extrusion	Normalized 4130 sheet		4130 H.T. to 125,000 psi
Thickness →	.010–.249	.050–.249	≦.187	>.187	As req'd
Ultimate tensile stress	59,000 psi	57,000 psi	95,000 psi	90,000 psi	125,000 psi
Yield tensile stress	39,000 psi	42,000 psi	75,000 psi	70,000 psi	103,000 psi
Compression yield stress	36,000 psi	38,000 psi	75,000 psi	70,000 psi	113,000 psi
Ultimate shear stress	38,000 psi	30,000 psi	55,000 psi	55,000 psi	82,000 psi
Ultimate bearing stress (2 dia. edge dist.)	114,000 psi	108,000 psi	200,000 psi	190,000 psi	251,000 psi
Weight, lb/cu in.	.10	.10	.30	.30	.30
e = elongation	12–15%	12%	10–15%	over 17%	10%

Figure 10-2 Comparative properties of aircraft materials (see Fig. 10-1 for materials specifications).

Material	Ultimate tensile stress, psi	Material hardness	
		Rockwell B 100 kg	Rockwell C 150 kg
ALUMINUM ALLOYS			
5052-H34	34,000	B15/B22	
5052-H38	39,000	B28/B38	
6061-T4	30,000	B3/B15	
6061-T6	42,000	B38/B45	
2024-T3	Bare 64,000	B72/B76	
	Alclad 59,000	B67/B72	
7075-T6	77,000	B82/B87	
STEEL ALLOYS			
1015-1025 mild steel	55,000	B64/B68	
4130A (annealed)	70-85,000	B77/B87	
4130N (normalized)	90-95,000	B90/B94	
4130-heat treated	125,000		C26/C30
4130-heat treated	150,000 max.		C33/C37
4340-heat treated	180,000		C39/C42

Figure 10-3 Materials and their hardness. Aluminum and steel alloys commonly used in aircraft construction.

be expected in view of the additional manufacturing process involved, alclad is slightly more expensive than bare material.

The main advantage of alclad sheet lies in the capability of the aluminum surface to (1) resist corrosion better than alloy material and (2) "flow over" and thereby seal minor surface scratches—which action, of course, protects the alloy core within. As a result, alclad sheet metal parts exhibit superior corrosion resistance compared to bare sheet, and increasingly so when alodined and primed prior to assembly—as should be done for seaplane structural components. A further advantage of alclad sheet is that it can be polished and kept clean without painting if you want a show plane, although this requires considerable elbow grease for proper maintenance and really has to be a labor of love. Regardless of whether the structure is to be painted, the corrosion resistance of alclad skins and parts increases the structural life and value of any airplane. The slight increase in cost is worthwhile provided the structure was originally designed for alclad material strength values.

If you are building with 4130 steel sheet or tubing in accordance with drawing specifications, I highly recommend that you bring no steel material *except* 4130 into your shop. The possibility of using 1020 steel where a critical 4130 steel part is required is just too potentially dangerous to warrant the slight saving involved in using 1020 for anything. Equally important, be sure to use only 4130 *normalized* (4130N) steel for the final 4130 steel part or assembly. Do not use annealed 4130 steel for any final items because of its low structural value, as shown in Figure 10-3. Annealed 4130 is little better than 1015–1025 (which includes 1020) mild steel and way below the intended strength for any 4130N part.

You may readily purchase 4130 sheet, bar, plate, and tubing in the normalized state if you so specify; bar and plate are also available as 125,000-lb/sq in heat treated stock. If you are not sure of the type or strength of certain material available in your shop or from a supply source, the Rockwell hardness values given in Figure 10-3 will help define its properties. A Rockwell test can be performed for you at any good machine shop or well-equipped aircraft maintenance and repair station. If hardness tests are frequently required, you can purchase a small Ames or similar hand-held hardness tester as one of your shop tools, but since new ones cost quite a few hundred dollars, they are hard to justify if you keep your materials well marked and properly segregated.

Sources for materials and hardware are listed in Reference 10.1 at the end of this chapter. In addition to these better-known companies, you probably have local suppliers for aluminum and steel who will be listed in the yellow pages of your classified telephone directory. If possible, buy locally; the freight you save will be considerable, and deliveries will frequently be much more rapid. But regardless of where or what you purchase, be sure to specify the *exact* material called for on the design drawings. If a substitution must be made, do not select an alternate without first receiving designer approval. This basic safety commandment cannot be repeated too often and must be scrupulously followed by all builders for their own future safety as well as that of their passengers.

PROCESSES

In addition to such standard processes as cadmium plating and steel heat treatment, which are usually better left to established shops, every homebuilder sooner or later is faced with the problems of corrosion prevention; heat treatment of aluminum alloys; and properly installing the fuel, hydraulic, and brake systems. These requirements are not only common to all aircraft but also basic to flight safety.

One of the best ways to prevent corrosion is through discouraging its occurrence right from the time the airplane is being assembled. The following materials classifications and assembly isolation procedures have been developed and tested over many years. If you follow them carefully, your airplane will have a longer and safer life and be of greater value as well.

Isolation of Dissimilar Materials for Aircraft Assembly

I. Definition of Dissimilar Metals (Ref. AND 10398)
   A. Group 1: magnesium and its alloys.
   B. Group 2: cadmium, zinc, aluminum, and their alloys.
   C. Group 3: iron, lead, tin, and their alloys, such as steel (except stainless steel).
   D. Group 4: copper, chromium, nickel, silver, gold, platinum, titanium, cobalt, rhodium, and their alloys; stainless steel; and graphite.

II. Rules
   A. Metals classified in the same group are considered similar to one another.
   B. Materials classified in different groups are considered dissimilar.
   C. This specification does not apply to standard attaching parts, such as rivets, bolts, nuts, and washers.
   D. For the purpose of this specification, the metal referred to is the metal on the surfaces of the part. For example, if zinc is referred to, it includes all-zinc parts, such as castings, as well as zinc-coated parts, whether the zinc coating is electrodeposited, applied by hot dipping, or by metal spraying over similar or dissimilar metal parts.
   E. When cadmium plated steel and aluminum parts are in contact, they are to be treated as dissimilar metals despite the fact that they are in the same group.

III. Treatment

A. For assembly of fabricated parts of different groups or per E above, each of the contacting surfaces shall be primed with zinc chromate primer and a layer of thin zinc chromate paste applied between the surfaces at the time the joint is being made. Fuller-O'Brien Corporation Compound No. 3997 is of the proper consistency for this application, as is their No. 8509 Slushing Compound.

B. Critical bolts, such as wing, tail, landing gear, engine mount, propeller, and float attachment, shall be dipped into zinc-chromate primer of spraying or brushing consistency immediately prior to assembly.

C. Wing fittings shall be isolated from structural frames and beam caps per A above. Attachment bolts shall be installed per B.

D. Seat track, floor board, and heater installation screw and bolt threads shall be given a light coating of waterproof grease or Parker Threadlube prior to installation.

Builders constructing all-metal aircraft requiring heat treatment of aluminum alloy parts formed in the annealed (O) condition frequently need to have a part heat treated before proceeding further. If a qualified aluminum heat treatment facility is not available within the general locality, stopping to ship parts away and waiting for their eventual return can prove most annoying. In addition to the time lost, heat treating is usually priced at a minimum-batch rate for each firing, meaning one piece can cost as much to harden as a hundred, depending upon the size and number of parts to be treated.

Because such interruptions rapidly increase construction time and cost, some builders have successfully made their own electrically fired small ovens, capable of handling a number of pieces in a single loading. A convenient size for treating pieces up to 4 ft long would be a cavity about 1 or 2 ft wide by 4 ft high and 3 to 4 ft deep. Since heat treat temperatures for aluminum alloy are not nearly as high as those for steel, calrod or similar heating elements will do the job, while oven temperatures can be thermostatically controlled with reasonably priced sensing units.

For builders who may wish to assemble a simple furnace, as well as for those curious about aluminum alloy heat treatment temperatures, the following process specifications should be of interest:

Aluminum Alloy Heat Treat Procedures

I. Aluminum 2024 per QQ-A-250/4 and -250/5

A. Condition O to T4: Heat treat sheet, plate, and rolled or drawn shapes at 920°F ± 10° for length of time indicated in Figure 10-4. Quench immediately in water at room temperature. Rockwell hardness B 69 to B 78.

B. Condition T4 or T3 to "O": Anneal heat treated parts at 775 °F ± 10° for 2 to 3 hr. Cool at a controlled rate of 50 °F per hr down to 500 °F, followed by uncontrolled cooling to room temperature.

II. Aluminum 6061 per QQ-A250/11

    A. Condition O to T4: Heat treat sheet, plate, and rolled or drawn shapes at 985 °F ± 10 °F for length of time indicated in Figure 10-4. Quench immediately in water at room temperature. Rockwell hardness B 3 to B 15.

    B. Condition T4 to T6: Heat treat at 320 °F ± 10 °F for 18 hr or at 350 °F ± 10° for 8 hr. Cool at room temperature. Rockwell hardness B 38 to B 45.

    C. Condition T4 or T6 to "O": Anneal heat treated parts at 775 °F for 2 to 3 hr. Cool at a controlled rate of 50 °F per hr down to 500 °F, followed by uncontrolled cooling to room temperature.

III. Aluminum 7075 per QQ-A-250/12 and -250/13

    A. Condition "O" to W: Heat treat at 900 °F ± 10 °F for length of time indicated in Figure 10–4. Quench immediately in water at room temperature.

    B. Condition W to T6: (a) Heat treat at 245 °F ± 10°7 for 3 hr, followed by 315 °F ± 10 °F for 3 hr or (b) 250 °F ± 10 °F for 24 hr. Cool at room temperature. Rockwell hardness B 82 to B 87.

    C. Condition W or T6 to "O": Anneal heat treated parts at 775 °F ± 10 °F for 2 to 3 hr, followed by uncontrolled cooling to 400 °F or less, followed by reheating to 450° ± 10 °F for 4 hr and uncontrolled cooling to room temperature.

Note that both temperature and time are critical. Aluminum alloy parts treated at too high a temperature or for too long a period will either become so brittle they shatter when dropped or just simply melt away into small puddles at the bottom of the furnace. If you build an aluminum alloy heat treatment furnace, be sure to test a few pieces of annealed scrap carefully before thrusting your precious formed parts into possible oblivion; and have these samples hardness tested as well, even if they do appear satisfactory.

Parts that have been heat treated from 0 to -T4 condition will remain soft for about one-half hour after quenching and can be further worked during that time. If it is necessary to keep treated parts pliable for some time before they can be worked, put them into a deep freezer at least 5 °F *below zero* as soon as they have cooled from quenching. This low temperature will keep heat treated parts pliable indefinitely or until you take them out for 20 minutes or so of rework. However, once out of the freezer for over one-half hour, sheet metal parts will be nearly in the -T4 condition and should not be worked further without being annealed and then, of course, reheat treated. This anneal-and-reheat treatment cycle can be repeated three or four

Minimum Thickness Heaviest Section	Length of Time in Furnace (min)	
	Minimum	Maximum Clad only
.016 and under	20	25
.017 – .020	20	30
.021 – .032	25	35
.033 – .063	30	40
.064 – .090	35	45
.091 – .125	40	55
.126 – .250	55	65
.251 – .500	65	75
.501 – 1.000	90	100
For each additional ½ in or fraction	Add 30 minutes	

Note: Times indicated start after furnace temperature is stabilized.

Figure 10-4 Heat-treat cycles for 2024, 6061, and 7075 aluminum. (*Alcoa Aluminum Handbook Table 12, p.62.*)

times if necessary, but with repeated cycling, parts tend to become increasingly brittle in the reannealed state.

Steel heat treatment and hardening requires such high furnace temperatures, plus properly controlled oil bath quenching facilities, that builders should plan to have steel parts hardened by an approved company specializing in this work. If possible, request certification of the treatment procedure, including the specification process and Rockwell hardness values.

Many homebuilt aircraft dead-stick landing and takeoff accidents are caused by clogged fuel lines. The use of improper compounds on fuel-line coupling and fitting threads is a major cause of such losses, as is incorrect application of these lubricants. To a less serious extent, the same comment applies equally well to brake lines that become leaky or blocked, causing brake failure at a critical moment as the end of the runway looms ever nearer during landing runout; and also to clogged hydraulic lines that will not lower the gear or flaps during approach.

The following procedures are offered as accepted methods of sealing joints with minimum risk of line blockage and should be considered during final assembly of your airplane.

Application of Fuel and Oil System Thread Seal and Antiseize Compound

1. Brush-on-type Tite Seal Gasket & Joint Sealing Compound #T35-04, nonhardening, shall be used on all fuel and oil system threaded fittings.

To prevent sealant from contaminating oil and fuel lines, care shall be taken that Tite Seal is not used in excessive amounts and is placed only on threaded surfaces. Tite Seal may be purchased from Radiator Specialty Company, 1400 West Independence Boulevard, Charlotte, NC 28201.

2. Use of Teflon tape is prohibited on all threads.

Application of Hydraulic-System Thread Seal and Antiseize Compound

1. Petrolatum (Spec. AN-P-51) or Parker-Hannifin Fuelube (Spec. MIL-L-6032 Amend. 1) shall be used as a thread seal and antiseize compound on all threaded connections in hydraulic and brake systems.

To prevent contaminating and blocking hydraulic lines, care shall be taken that compound is not used in excessive amounts and is placed only on threaded surfaces.

2. Neither Parker Sealube or Threadlube should be used with hydraulic and brake system fluids.

FINISHES

As noted in the materials discussion, alclad sheet can be left bright, but the resulting polishing maintenance may soon prove unacceptable. Continued polishing may also be undesirable as the thin aluminum surface can be worn away, leaving the alloy core exposed to weather and corrosion.

Surface Preparation

If parts of all-metal aircraft are not individually alodined and primed prior to assembly, surfaces can be corrosion-protected and prepared for finish painting either by washing with an alodine solution and then priming or by spraying with a wash primer.

Automobile supply stores carrying finish paints usually stock or will order surface preparation and alodine solutions in small quantities suitable for homebuilder use. These materials are:

1. Amchem Alumiprep No. 33, Stock No. DX533-¼ (Alumiprep No. 44 is also acceptable). This is 1 qt of surface degreaser and cleaner that is diluted with water and applied to the surface before using the second solution which is:

2. Amchem Alodine 1201 Stock No. DX503. This is the chemical coating for aluminum.

Directions for application are clearly stamped on each container. Small parts can be alodine-protected by immersing them in a plastic bucket containing the solution, while complete skins can be alodined by treating them individually prior to or after assembly. Either way, alodined surfaces should be given a coat of zinc chromate or epoxy primer prior to applying finish paint.

Wash primer treatment consists of a two-part solution which etches the aluminum surface to provide corrosion protection and also acts as a base for finish paint. It must be prepared immediately before use and applied by paint spray gun. Any solution left over cannot be saved for reuse since wash primer tends to separate and become stringy if left standing after mixing. In fact, the spray gun, hoses, and all containers should be thoroughly cleaned immediately after use to prevent clogging. Acceptable wash primers are available from Randolph Products Company, listed in Reference 10.1.

The importance of alodine and primer or wash-primer finishes is twofold in that either process provides increased corrosion protection plus an excellent base for the finish paint, which, of course, provides the initial corrosion-protection barrier.

Finish Paints

There are so many finish paints and processes available for fabric, wooden, or all-metal airplanes that you can be easily overwhelmed by the challenge of selection. Imron, by du Pont, is excellent for all-metal surfaces properly prepared for this finish; many other acceptable paints are available from Randolph Products and other general aviation suppliers included in the list of sources at the end of this chapter. Randolph also has bulletins with instructions for finishing different types of aircraft exteriors (and interiors) available for the asking, as has du Pont for the Imron process.

Although enamels and lacquers have been around for years, the enamels have recently branched into acrylic and polyurethane bases as well as the old standard type—each with its own group of enthusiasts. Polyurethane may be the easier to apply because of its fairly long pot life, but both acrylic and polyurethane enamels are two-part paints requiring an activator plus the use of stir pots during spraying. Either may be hot-sprayed for a fast drying finish and will provide excellent protection with a high gloss. So take your choice.

For fast backyard or hangar repairs, lacquer is easy to apply and offers adequate protection when the base coat is sound. Plain old 4-hour drying enamel will probably last longer, offer a higher gloss finish, and may be applied over any paint. Remember that lacquer cannot be applied over enamel; it will attack the surface and immediately develop a crinkle finish.

Although the choice of paint will probably depend upon the color match available, finish paint provides important protection for the airframe. Any scratches or local peeling should be covered as soon as possible, even if primer is the only finish readily available.

Scratches or gouges in a fiber-glass structure should also be given immediate attention because it is possible for water to work between the glass layers. This moisture may either expand as trapped steam when the airplane is parked in intense sunlight or freeze and crack the structure locally during exposure to low ambient temperatures. Fiber-glass repair kits are available for quick touch-up jobs and should be used as soon as possible after surface defects are noticed.

Automobile body filler will smooth metal and fiber-glass surfaces when local dents or gouges cannot be worked out and should be applied in just the same manner minor auto body repairs are made at home. A better and lighter material is a form of fiber-glass filler known as Feather Fill, available from the source noted in Reference 10.2. This filler may be sprayed or troweled in place on metal or fiber glass, sanded smooth, and then finish-painted. The smoother the sanding job, the better the surface; unfortunately, much elbow grease is essential to all good finish work.

Seaplane Protection

Seaplanes likely to operate in salt water must have special protection in addition to exterior paint. When possible, all aluminum-alloy parts should be fabricated from alclad sheet, alodined, and primed. Control cables should be of 7 × 19 stainless steel, specification MIL-C-5424 or MIL-W-83420, for maximum life and strength. All exterior cables should be coated with Par-Al-Ketone and touched up as often as necessary to maintain a continuous coating.

All interior and exterior bolt heads, nuts, and bolt ends should also have a brush coating of Par-Al-Ketone, with interior bolts and nuts given an additional seal of Vaseline if located down low in bilge areas. This represents a lot of work, but so does replacement of badly corroded fittings. And stainless bolts or screws, contrary to popular belief, are not an acceptable substitute for cad-plated steel AN (Air Force-Navy Standard Hardware) bolts in aluminum-alloy structures exposed to salt water. I learned this the hard way a few years ago when I finally had to chisel and drill out a steel bolt which, in one sailing season, had become frozen (corroded) into the extruded aluminum mast of my ocean racing sailboat. Galvanized dip-plated steel parts really behave best around aluminum and salt water, but the plating is so soft and irregular in texture that galvanized bolts are not acceptable for joining highly stressed structural members.

With constant attention and a quick check of critical areas after each water flight, the special problems of saltwater operation should not demand excessive maintenance. Probably the most effective corrosion inhibitor of all is a thorough wash down with fresh water immediately after each briny dip. If washing is not possible, fly to a nearby freshwater lake or river and run through two or three landings (gear-up, if an amphibian); this is not as satisfactory as a good hosing but much better than nothing.

When all is said and done, keeping your airplane clean and polished contributes the most toward a lasting finish; and, of course, the smoother the surface, the lower the skin friction drag—and better the performance. A polished airplane also reflects pride of ownership.

So you personally gain all around if you can treat routine and finish maintenance the same way you would any pleasant hobby. The only way you can then improve upon caring for your airplane is by keeping it hangared. Being under cover is the ultimate way to increase the life of the entire airplane—in addition to assuring a lasting finish.

REFERENCES

10.1 Sources for Aircraft Hardware and Materials

Aircraft Spruce and Specialty Company, P.O, Box 424, Fullerton, CA 92632. The Sears Roebuck of homebuilt aircraft for hardware and materials with a good record of service.

Aviation Products, Inc., 114 Bryant, Ojai, CA 93023. Hardware, sealing compounds, instruments, supplies, etc., but no materials.

B & F Aircraft Supply Inc., 6141 West 95 Street, Oak Lawn, IL 60453. Hardware, instruments, supplies and materials, engines.

Fibre-Glass Developments, 1944 Neva Drive, Dayton, OH 45414. Source of all fiber glass, epoxy, polyester, Kevlar, and carbon fiber requirements. Specializes in mail order, and provides rapid service.

General Aerospace Materials Corporation, 93 East Bethpage Road, Plainview, NY 11803. Major supplier of aircraft metals, including aluminum sheet, plate, bar and extrusions as well as steel tubing and bar. Used to dealing with major aerospace companies and has a minimum order value. Even so, carries almost everything you could want. No catalogue.

J & M Aircraft Supply Inc., P.O. Box 7586, Shreveport, LA 71107.

Randolph Products Company, P.O. Box 67, Carlstadt, NJ 07072. Aircraft paints and finishes. Also good source for finish bulletins.

Spar Craft Manufacturing Company, 106 South 15 Street, Tacoma, WA 98402. Supplier of wood kits for a number of aircraft. These kits are especially suited for builders who want to do all of their own woodwork but prefer not to saw and mill all of the wood involved.

Stan Weiss Enterprises, 761 East Brokaw Road, San Jose, CA 95112. Supplies kits of fabricated wood components with an excellent reputation for workmanship.

Tiernay Metals, 2600 Compton Boulevard, Redondo Beach, CA 90278. Aerospace extrusions only and is the best source, providing you need a reasonable amount. Not used to dealing with homebuilders.

Trimcraft Aero, 6254 Highway 36, Burlington, WI 53105. In the aircraft wood business and has a full line of spruce and plywood, as well as other materials.

Wag-Aero, Inc., P.O. Box 181, 1216 North Road, Lyons, WI 53148. CUBy homebuilt; source of radios and parts.

Wicks Aircraft Supply, Madison County, Highland, IL 62249. Good source for spruce, plywood, and other materials.

Wil Neubert Aircraft Supply, P.O. Box 46, Arroyo Grande, CA 93420. Hardware, instruments, components, and so on. An excellent reputation.

Williams & Company, 901 Pennsylvania Avenue, Pittsburgh, PA 15233. Major industrial supplier of steel and aluminum. No catalogue.

10.2 Feather Fill is available in pint, quart, and gallon quantities from Fibre Glass-Evercoat Company, Inc., 6600 Cornell Road, Cincinnati, OH 45242.

part *FOUR*

Flying and Maintenance Considerations

chapter ELEVEN

Homebuilder Insurance

Once your airplane is ready for flight, liability insurance is essential. While it is advisable to provide increasing amounts of fire protection as construction work progresses, it is mandatory that adequate liability coverage be in force when that critical first flight finally occurs. In view of the sizable investments in time and money committed over the past few years, hull insurance, which covers damage to your airplane, should also be obtained prior to trailing a completed airplane to the airport.

The availability of liability and hull coverage will vary according to your individual pilot qualifications and ratings, your hours of flying time and years of flight experience, your past safety record, and, to a large extent, the type of airplane you have built. By "type of airplane," I mean the specific design, which in turn relates most importantly to the experience record of that particular model: how many have been built, their safety record, the likely range of damage repair costs (as regards hull coverage), and similar considerations.

A number of companies will insure homebuilt aircraft, although a greater number will not. Avemco (see Ref. 11.1) is one agency which actively seeks homebuilder insurance business to the extent of advertising in EAA's *Sport Aviation* magazine. For approved builders, Avemco's hull policy includes an allowance of $5 per hour for self-repair labor if a policyholder's aircraft should be damaged, provided Avemco has agreed to the owner's bid estimate and approved the owner as qualified to perform the repair work. In addition, for most designs, Avemco liability coverage includes all passengers as well as the usual third-party protection limits.

The picture may not be all this bright, however, for a builder completing a relatively untried new model—particularly if the builder has little previous flight time and possibly only a private license with no additional ratings such as seaplane or instrument flight. In view of this, during the winter of 1979–1980 I corresponded with Tom Poberezny, executive vice president of the EAA, concerning the possible extent of EAA's interest in supporting homebuilder insurance and to inquire whether builders had written to EAA for assistance in finding necessary insurance coverage. His reply follows:

> I have found that there are a number of companies offering insurance to homebuilders, but each policy varies drastically. I have found that most agents dealing with

the amateur builder charge a high premium in order to protect themselves because they do not understand the program. In some cases the builder thinks he has insurance protection that he does not really have.

EAA is in the process of developing a master insurance policy for all members. This policy would provide liability and hull insurance coverage, non-owned aircraft insurance coverage, life insurance, etc. It would also provide insurance coverage for a project that is under construction. This program would be available only to EAA members. The reason that we are developing this is because of the numerous and varied policies appearing across the country. We ran a study through *Sport Aviation,* and it was amazing the response that we had in terms of "homebuilt insurance."

In your letter you asked whether or not we receive letters from members who have had difficulty in finding insurance. The answer to that is, without a doubt, yes. We have not found too much of a difference between landplanes and seaplanes, mainly because the majority of homebuilt aircraft are landplanes.

I'm glad that you brought forth the insurance question. In today's society it is one that is very important; for not having liability insurance, hull insurance, etc., allows one to be potentially financially strapped in the event of a mishap. We feel that our EAA insurance program should be put together within the next 2 to 3 months and that an announcement will be made to that effect sometime this spring or early summer [of 1980 —author].

Subsequent conversation confirmed that EAA has developed a policy protecting homebuilt aircraft under construction as well as providing liability and hull insurance coverage during ground and flight operation after completion. This program was expected to be operational in 1980 at considerably lower cost for EAA members than previously available aircraft insurance. Even so, premium rates will vary depending upon the type of airplane insured, the hours flown per year, and pilot experience.

In conclusion, it is most important to realize that if you are unable to obtain liability coverage because of your lack of experience or the airplane design you have selected, you are really risking all you own each time you fly. With court decisions in liability suits being what they are today, no one can justify operating without sufficient liability protection to cover her or his net worth. The logical solution is to make sure ahead of time that you will be able to obtain the necessary insurance coverage when you need it, even if it means that you must fly during the construction period in order to have sufficient experience by the anticipated flight date (or year). As an equally important corollary, before starting construction, inquire and make sure the airplane model you intend to build will not *preclude* insurance coverage at a reasonable premium regardless of how much experience or how excellent a record you may have. Since there is little joy in spending 2 to 5 years building something you will not be able to fly, the question of insurance looms larger than first thought would indicate and should be resolved before construction begins.

REFERENCES

II.I Avemco Insurance Company, 7315 Wisconsin Avenue, Bethesda, MD 20014.

You can't believe it! After all that time and effort, your own personal creation is ready for flight. Insurance has been taken care of, including insurance for this first-ever trip around the pattern; the weather is calm and clear; everyone has turned out to witness the event; and a celebration is planned for after the wheels return to earth—or the hull to water, as the case may be.

But before turning your new airplane loose in this first flight which seemed so far away for so many years, schedule a few hours additional delay for a thorough pre-flight inspection. The following list contains possible danger areas that should be expanded and set down in table form as necessary to support a thorough preflight inspection of your airplane. Based upon FAA reports of conditions found on new and low-time aircraft, this series of troublemakers appears hair-raising at first sight but, once a check has been run and all items found in place and secure, can be a source of security.

Aileron control cable not over pulley.

Aileron cable improperly installed in bell crank.

Bolt installed backwards at the flap cable attachment to the flap.

Bolts loose on the vertical and horizontal stabilizer beam attachments.

Broken and cracked electrical terminals.

Control cable turnbuckles not safetied.

Flap follow-up cable chafing on brake line.

Foreign items in fuel cells or tanks.

Fuel lines twisted, bent, or kinked obstructing flow.

Fuel lines chafing—inadequate clamping.

Incorrect propeller bolts installed.

Jam nuts drilled, but no safety wire installed.

Lock clips missing from control cable turnbuckles.

Loose rivets in horizontal stabilizer leading edge.

Main wheel tires do not clear wheel bays during retraction.

Oil lines leaking at connection.

Primer line "T" fitting not installed.

Propeller blade retention ferrules undertorqued.

Right elevator trim cable wrapped around right primary rudder control cable (check all cables).

Rivet holes drilled, but rivets not installed in different areas.

Rudder cable bell crank attach bolts loose.

Rudder cable bolts fitted upside down.

Unreliable fuel quantity indication.

Plugged airspeed and fuel vent lines.

Surface controls improperly connected and giving opposite surface action.

Not to be a wet blanket, but rather to keep the first-flight event a happy one, a bit of soul-searching is also in order before getting into the cockpit for that initial takeoff. Do you really have the flying experience plus sufficiently rapid and trained reflexes to cope with an unexpected situation in flight—such as a severe out-of-trim condition (wing alignment, tail setting, incorrect center of gravity location, and so on); powerplant failure (fuel line blockage or breakage, loss of propeller, jammed engine controls, crankshaft failure, or similar); loss of airspeed indication; loss of lift as speed is reduced; and similar delightful happenings? Since you are not as young as you were when the building program began, do you still want to dash into the air and possibly risk all your work?

If the answers to these questions seem a bit delayed or are negative, I recommend that you hire a professional pilot or get an experienced pilot friend to make the first flight. You can delight in seeing how your airplane looks from the ground; if you will be doing all the flying from now on, this may be your only chance to admire your own work in action. You can complete the preflight taxi and fuel system run-up checks and possibly make a few high-speed runs ending in 1- to 2-ft lift-offs so you will not miss all the fun, but I personally believe that just as doctors do not normally treat members of their immediate families in order to preclude possible emotional involvement, builders should not make the first flight in their own airplanes. When something goes wrong, builders will tend to save the airplane rather than do what is necessary to save themselves, which might require a controlled crash into trees or bailing out at altitude with complete loss of the airplane.

This brings up my second recommendation: do not fly the first 10 hours without wearing a recently packed parachute plus shoulder harness. In fact, wear shoulder harnesses every time you and your passengers fly thereafter.

My third recommendation is probably obvious: assuming your homebuilt has two or more seats, there should only be one person in the airplane during the initial flight and until at least 5 hours have been flown off.

As a final safety consideration: in addition to the required flight and powerplant instruments, I believe every homebuilt airplane should be equipped with a cylinder-head temperature gauge on the hottest cylinder. Determining this position may require checking every cylinder in flight. In the process, if the temperature spread between cylinders is too great, cooling can be reworked as necessary by rebaffling or changing the cowling inlet/outlet areas. I offer this recommendation because homebuilt cowlings are sometimes modified and styled to suit the eye of the builder, frequently resulting in cooling air starvation, engine overheating, loss of power, and a dead-stick landing. By establishing cooling within the manufacturer's proscribed limits and then monitoring operation to keep it that way, you will prolong the life of your engine and possibly your own as well (see Ref. 8.3).

FAA regulations limit flights of new homebuilt aircraft to the comparative safety of the local airport for the first 25 hours of operation, after which limited cross-country travel is permitted for the next 25 hours. Presumably all bugs will be flown off or have gone away by the fiftieth hour of operation because the FAA permits unrestricted flight after that time for aircraft powered by a certified engine and propeller. Homebuilts using uncertified engines require 75 hours of flight before restrictions are lifted. It should also be noted that even with FAA restrictions removed, travel over the border is a bit more complex for "experimental aircraft," as all homebuilts are labeled, usually requiring special foreign approval to fly a "Made in USA" homebuilt outside the United States and vice versa.

If you carefully consider who should first fly your new airplane, get a complete checkout and a few hours of flight time in a similar airplane if the design has two or more seats, and fly sufficiently frequently to remain proficient, your airplane should provide you with years of trouble-free enjoyment and endless conversation. You have spent many hours building your airplane; now plan to spend an equal amount of time flying it safely.

chapter THIRTEEN

Keeping Airworthy

The safety record of registered homebuilt aircraft was briefly reviewed in Chapter 4 and found comparable to that of certified production types. As further described in Reference 13.1, about 4 percent of all licensed small aircraft are involved in accidents every year. The fact that homebuilts are as safe as production models is a tribute to their designers and builders as well as to their pilots.

Every year many forums concerned with improving the safety record, including both recommended construction and operational procedures, are heavily attended at EAA's annual convention in Oshkosh as well as during other major EAA regional gatherings held in Lakeland, Florida; Chino, California; and Tullahoma, Tennessee. Ranging from open discussion sessions to more formal design lectures, these forums are conducted by volunteer EAA members who are experienced mechanics, pilots, and design engineers active in the homebuilt field. Advice picked up at these meetings has reduced construction time and cost for many builders while, at the same time, actively contributing to an improved homebuilt safety record. Safety tips are also carried in each issue of EAA's *Sport Aviation* magazine, which alone returns the cost of annual membership many times over.

Absorbing information by listening and reading is not enough; it must be practiced to be effective. Safety starts with the pilot, and so it is mandatory that you remain flight-proficient while also keeping your airplane in top condition. Although what constitutes being "flight proficient" can vary from pilot to pilot, most flight instructors and examiners agree that flying 1 hour per week is barely enough. However, 45 hours per year is the average time logged by Aircraft Owners and Pilots Association (AOPA) member pilots, so many must fly fewer than 1 hour per week while still considering themselves to be active. Flying for pleasure is expensive—which is one reason you decided to build your own airplane; now that you have it, use it by flying at least 3 to 5 hours per week as weather permits.

Assuming that you will keep airworthy, it is equally important that your airplane be kept that way as well. Again the responsibility falls upon the owner, both legally to satisfy the FAA and from the standpoint of personal safety.

A thorough preflight inspection—including a physical check of the fuel levels in each tank and all control surface hinge points as well as more routine items—is particularly recommended for homebuilt aircraft. Since many designs may be relatively new and have accumulated little service time, it is mandatory that any component critical to flight be inspected frequently, and control surfaces certainly fall into that category. Your particular airplane may have other items that should be watched for the first year or so; making a detailed preflight checklist and carefully following it every time you fly is the best way to keep flying. While it may be a cliché, there is much truth to the comment that "there are no old, bold, or careless pilots." Thorough preflight inspections are practiced by military pilots and airline captains, regardless of their ground-crew support, thus setting a safety example to be followed by all private pilots.

Thanks in large part to the effort of Paul Poberezny, president of the EAA, it is now possible for homebuilders to perform the FAA-required annual inspection on their own airplanes. This privilege has been based in part upon recognition that persons who build their own aircraft are probably best qualified to maintain them in airworthy condition. This philosophy shines like a guiding light and represents a practical approach to servicing the growing fleet of homebuilt aircraft. It also saves the homebuilder considerable money every year. But in return, every builder assumes the responsibility to maintain and service his or her airplane properly. The requirements of this new privilege are defined by the FAA in Advisory Circular 65-23 (see Ref. 13.2) as follows:

1. Effective September 10, 1979, experimental certificates issued for homebuilt aircraft have an unlimited duration. However, FAA inspectors will continue to perform the original certification inspection (during construction and prior to first flight).

2. Each homebuilder may be certified as a repairman* approved to perform airplane condition inspections (this covers annual inspections).

3. Builders desiring to be certificated as a repairman must make application for a repairman certificate at the time of original certification of their airplane.

4. It is necessary that the builder applicant for repairman certificate be a U.S. citizen or permanent resident of 18 years of age, and also "demonstrate to the certifying FAA inspector his or her ability to perform condition inspections and to determine whether the subject aircraft is in a condition for safe operation."

5. Copies of the necessary Rating Application, FAA Form 8610-2 (OMB 04-R0065), may be obtained from the FAA General Aviation District Office (GADO) or Flight Standards District Office. The completed form is to be submitted to your local FAA office for consideration.

*FAA terminology

Advisory Circulars 20-27B and 20-28A (see Refs. 13.3 and 13.4) cover aircraft kit and homebuilt certification requirements. With some effort on your part, not only will you have a special one-of-a-kind airplane, but the FAA will also permit you to perform all service and repair functions necessary to keep it airworthy. With full support of the designers, suppliers, and FAA available for the asking, when do you start building? Is tomorrow too soon?

I sincerely hope this book has thoroughly aroused your interest in building your own airplane. Few hobbies can offer so much creative satisfaction, personal enjoyment, and social contact. And all this is topped off by the fact that a well-constructed homebuilt airplane usually has a market value well in excess of any capital investment. With such a positive combination, how can you lose? See you at Oshkosh next year!

REFERENCES

13.1 David B. Thurston, *Design for Safety*, McGraw-Hill, New York, 1980, pp. 14–17.

13.2 FAA Advisory Circular, AC 65-23. *Certification of Repairmen (Experimental Aircraft Builders)*, September 28, 1979. Available from local FAA offices or U.S. Department of Transportation, Publications Section, M-443.1, Washington, DC 20591.

13.3 FAA Advisory Circular, AC 20-27B. *Certification and Operation of Amateur-Built Aircraft*, April 20, 1972. Ibid.

13.4 FAA Advisory Circular, AC 20-28A. *Nationally Advertised Construction Kits, Amateur-Built Aircraft*, December 29, 1972. Ibid.

Index

Aerobatic category and pilots, 20, 25, 138
Aircamper, 20
Aircraft designs (by company or designer):
  Ace Aircraft Mfg. Co.:
    Flaglor Scooter, 42
    Model D Baby Ace, 41
    Model E Junior Ace, 41
  Acro Sport, Inc.:
    Acro Sport, 44
    Pober Pixie, 43
    Super Acro, 44
  Aerosport, Incorporated, Scamp, 45
  Aircraft Specialities Co.:
    Beta Bird, 47
    Wing Ding II, 46
  American Eagle Corporation, Eaglet, 110
  Anderson, Kingfisher, 121
  Andreasson:
    BA-4B, 48
    BA-11, 49
    MFI-9B, 50
  Barney Oldfield Aircraft Company, Baby Lakes (Baby
      Great Lakes), 51
  Bede Four Sales, Inc., BD-4, 52
  Bowers:
    Bi-Baby, 53
    Fly Baby, 53
  Brokaw Aviation, Inc., Bullet, 54
  Bryan Aircraft, Inc.:
    HP 18, 111
    HP 19, 112
  Bushby Aircraft, Inc.:
    MM-1 Midget Mustang, 55
    Mustang II, 55
  Catto Aircraft, Goldwing, 129
  Christen Industries, Inc., Eagle 1, 56
  Cvjetkovic:
    CA-65, 57
    CA-65A Skyfly, 57
  D'Apuzzo, Model D-260 Senior Aero Sport, 58
  Davis, Model DA-2A, 59

Aircraft designs (by company or designer) (Cont.):
  Durand Associates, Inc., Mark V, 60
  Evans Aircraft, VP-1, 61
  Fike, Model E, 62
  Franklin Manufacturing Corporation, Hummer,
      130
  Hillman Helicopters, Inc., Hornet, 107
  Hoefelmann, Schatzie, 149–152
  Javelin Aircraft Company, Inc., Wichawk, 63
  Jeffair, Barracuda, 64
  Jodel Aircraft (Avions Jodel):
    D92 Bebe, 65
    D150 Grand Tourisme, 65
  Jurca:
    MJ-2 Tempete, 66
    MJ-5 Sirocco, 68
    MJ-3, 67
  Kelly:
    Hatz CB-1, 69
    Kelly-D, 70
  Marquart, MA-5 Charger, 71
  Mitchell, U-2 Superwing, 131
  Monnett Experimental Aircraft, Inc.:
    Monerai P, 114
    Monerai S, 113
    Sonerai 1, 72
  Osprey Aircraft, Osprey 2, 122
  Pazmany Aircraft Corporation:
    PL-2, 73
    PL-4A, 74
  Piel:
    C.P. 60 Diamant and Super-Diamant, 75
    C.P. 328 Super-Emeraude, 76
  Pitts Aerobatics:
    S-1D Special, 77
    S-2 Series, 78
  Practavia Ltd., Sprite, 79
  Pterodactyl, Fledgling, 132
  Quickie Aircraft Corporation, Quickie, 80
  Redfern & Sons, Fokker Dr-1 replica, 145
  Replica Plans, SE-5A, 146

Aircraft designs (by company or designer) (*Cont.*):
  Rotec Engineering, Inc.:
    Powered Easy Riser, 133
    Rally 2, 133
  Rotor Way Aircraft, Inc., Scorpion 133, 108
  Rutan Aircraft Factory:
    Long-EZ, 82
    VariEze, 82
    VariViggen, 81
  Schweizer Aircraft Corporation, 2-33AK, 115
  Sequoia Aircraft Corporation:
    F.8L Falco, 85
    Model 300 Sequoia, 83
    Model 302 Kodiak, 84
  Sidewinder Corporation, Sidewinder, 86
  Smith's, Miniplane, 87
  Sorrell Aviation, SNS-7 Hiperbipe, 88
  Spencer Amphibian Air Car, S-12-E Air Car, 123
  Spratt and Company, Inc., Control Wing, 124
  Steen Aerolab, Inc., Skybolt, 89
  Stewart Aircraft Corporation, Headwind, 90
  Stolp Starduster Corporation:
    SA500 Starlet, 92
    SA700 Acroduster 1, 92
    SA750 Acroduster Too, 93
    Starduster Too, 91
  Striplin Aircraft Corporation, Flac, 134
  Taylor:
    Coot, 125
    Mini-Imp, 94
  Thorp Engineering Company, T-18, 95
  Thurston Aeromarine Corporation, TA 16 Trojan Amphibian, 126
  Ultraflight Inc., Lazair, 135
  Ultralight Flying Machines of Wisconsin, Powered UFM Easy Riser, 136
  Van's Aircraft:
    RV-3, 96
    RV-4, 97
    RV-6, 97
  Vintage Sailplane Association:
    Grunau Baby II, 147
    Ross R-3, 148
    WPB-1, Flying Plank, 116
  Volmer Aircraft:
    VJ-11 Solo, 117
    VJ-22, Sportsman, 127
    VJ-23, Swingwing, 118
    VJ-24E powered Sunfun, 119
  Wag-Aero, Inc.:
    Cuby Sport Trainer, 98
    Wag-A-Bond, 98
  Watson, Windwagon, 99

Aircraft designs (by company or designer) (*Cont.*):
  Weedhopper of Utah, Inc., JC-24-B Weedhopper, 137
  Western Aircraft Supplies, PGK-1 Hirondelle, 100
  Wittman, W-8 Tailwind, 101
  Zenair Ltd.:
    CH 100 Mono Z, 102
    CH 200 Zenith, 103
    CH 300 Tri Z, 104
  Zimmerman, Stephens Akro Model B, 105
  (*See also* Design considerations)
Aircraft designs (by model):
  Acroduster 1 SA700 (Stolp Starduster Corporation), 92
  Acroduster Too SA750 (Stolp Starduster Corporation), 93
  Acro Sport (Acro Sport, Inc.), 44
  Air Car S-12-E (Spencer Amphibian Air Car), 123
  BA-4B (Andreasson), 48
  BA-11 (Andreasson), 49
  Baby Ace D (Ace Aircraft Mfg. Co.), 41
  Baby Lakes (Baby Great Lakes) (Barney Oldfield Aircraft Company), 51
  Barracuda (Jeffair), 64
  BD-4 (Bede Four Sales, Inc.), 52
  Beta Bird (Aircraft Specialties Co.), 47
  Bi-Baby (Bowers), 53
  Bullet (Brokow Aviation, Inc.), 54
  CA65 (Cvjetkovic), 57
  CA65A Skyfly (Cvjetkovic), 57
  CH 100 Mono Z (Zenair Ltd.), 102
  CH 200 Zenith (Zenair Ltd.), 103
  CH 300 Tri Z (Zenair Ltd.), 104
  Control Wing (Spratt and Company, Inc.), 124
  Coot (Taylor), 125
  C.P. 60 Diamant (Avions Claude Piel), 75
  C.P. 328 Super-Emeraude (Avions Claude Piel), 76
  Cuby Sport Trainer (Wag-Aero, Inc.), 98
  D92 Bebe [Jodel Aircraft (Avions Jodel)], 65
  D150 Grand Tourisme [Jodel Aircraft (Avions Jodel)], 65
  Davis DA-2A (Davis), 59
  Durand Mark V (Durand Associates, Inc.), 60
  Eagle 1 (Christen Industries, Inc.), 56
  Eaglet (American Eagle Corporation), 110
  Easy Riser (powered) (Rotec Engineering, Inc.), 133
  Easy Riser (powered UFM) (Ultralight Flying Machines of Wisconsin), 136
  F.8L Falco (Sequoia Aircraft Corporation), 85
  Fike E (Fike), 62
  Flac (Striplin Aircraft Corporation), 134
  Flaglor Scooter (Ace Aircraft Mfg. Co.), 42
  Fledgling (Pterodactyl), 132
  Fly Baby (Bowers), 53
  Fokker Dr-1 replica (Redfern & Sons), 145
  Goldwing (Catto Aircraft), 129
  Grunau Baby II (Vintage Sailplane Association), 147

Aircraft designs (by model) (*Cont.*):
Hatz CB-1 (Kelly), 69
Headwind (Stewart Aircraft Corporation), 90
Hiperbipe SNS-7 (Sorrell Aviation), 88
Hirondelle PGK-1 (Western Aircraft Supplies), 100
Hornet (Hillman Helicopters, Inc.), 107
HP 18 (Bryan Aircraft, Inc.), 111
HP 19 (Bryan Aircraft, Inc.), 112
Hummer (Franklin Manufacturing Corporation), 130
Junior Ace E (Ace Aircraft Mfg. Co.), 41
Kelly-D (Kelly), 70
Kingfisher (Anderson), 121
Kodiak 302 (Sequoia Aircrft Corporation), 84
Lazair (Ultraflight Inc.), 135
Long-EZ (Rutan Aircraft Factory), 82
MA-5 Charger (Marquart), 71
MFI-9B (Andreasson), 50
MJ-2 Tempte (Jurca), 66
MJ-5 Sirocco (Jurca), 68
Midget Mustang I (Bushby Aircraft, Inc.), 55
Midget Mustang II (Bushby Aircraft, Inc.), 55
Mini-Imp (Taylor), 94
Miniplane (Smith), 87
MJ-3 (Jurca), 67
Monerai P (Monnett Experimental Aircraft, Inc.), 114
Monerai S (Monnett Experimental Aircraft, Inc.), 113
Mustang (Midget Mustang MM-1) (Bushby Aircraft, Inc.), 55
Mustang (Midget Mustang II) (Bushby Aircraft, Inc.), 55
Osprey 2 (Osprey Aircraft), 122
PL-2 (Pazmany Aircraft Corporation), 73
PL-4A (Pazmany Aircraft Corporation), 73
Pober Pixie (Acro Sport, Inc.), 43
Quickie (Quickie Aircraft Corporation), 80
Rally 2 (Rotec Engineering, Inc.), 133
Ross R-3 (Vintage Sailplane Association), 148
RV-3 (Van's Aircraft), 96
RV-4 (Van's Aircraft), 97
RV-6 (Van's Aircraft), 97
S-1D Special (Pitts Aerobatics), 77
S-2 Pitts (Pitts Aerobatics), 78
Scamp (Aerosport, Incorporated), 45
Schatzie (Hoefelmann), 149–152
Schweizer 2-33AK (Schweizer Aircraft Corporation), 115
Scorpion 133 (Rotor Way Aircraft, Inc.), 108
SE-5A (Replica Plans), 146
Senior Aero Sport D-260 (D'Apuzzo), 58
Sequoia 300 (Sequoia Aircraft Corporation), 83
Sidewinder (Sidewinder Corporation), 86
Skybolt (Steen Aero Lab, Inc.), 89
Sonerai 1 (Monnett Experimental Aircraft, Inc.), 72
Sprite (Practavia Ltd.), 79
Starduster Too (Stolp Starduster Corporation), 91

Aircraft designs (by model) (*Cont.*):
Starlet SA 500 (Stolp Starduster Corporation), 92
Stephens Akro B (Zimmerman), 105
Super Acro (Acro Sport, Inc.), 44
Tailwind W-8 (Wittman), 101
Thorp T-18 (Thorp Engineering Company), 95
Trojan TA16 Amphibian (Thurston Aeromarine Corporation), 126
U-2 Superwing (Mitchell Aircraft Corporation), 131
VariEze (Rutan Aircraft Factory), 82
VariViggen (Rutan Aircraft Factory), 81
VJ-11 Solo (Volmer Aircraft), 117
VJ-22 Sportman (Volmer Aircraft), 127
VJ-23 Swingwing (Volmer Aircraft), 118
VJ-24E powered Sunfun (Volmer Aircraft), 119
VP-1 (Evans Aircraft), 61
Wag-A-Bond (Wag-Aero, Inc.), 98
Weedhopper JC-24-B (Weedhopper of Utah, Inc.), 137
Wichawk (Javelin Aircraft Company, Inc.), 63
Windwagon (Watson), 99
Wing Ding II (Aircraft Specialties Co.), 46
WPB-1 Flying Plank (Vintage Sailplane Association), 116
(*See also* Design consideration)
Aircraft Owners and Pilots Association (AOPA), 201
Aircraft and Powerplant (A&P) license, 32, 38
Airframe, definition of, 39
Airport requirements, 35, 36, 138
Airworthiness, 201–203
Alclad (aluminum alloy), 179, 182
All-metal construction, 29, 32–33, 120, 174, 179, 183–184, 187, 189
Alloys:
aluminum, 7, 179–182, 184–186
steel, 180–182, 186
Aluminum alloys, 7, 179–182, 184–186
Amphibians, 35, 120–127
Angle of attack (AOA) indicator, 36
Annual International Convention and Sport Aviation Exhibition organized by EAA ("Oshkosh"), 5, 8, 12, 16, 18, 22, 23, 25, 37, 201
aircraft types attending, 37
Antique aircraft, 8, 15, 17–20, 22, 139–148
Antique Airplane Association (AAA), 15, 18, 22
Approved Type Certificate (ATC), 18
Automotive engines, 24, 34, 166, 168–169
Average amateur rating (NASAD), 17

Books and manuals, aircraft construction, 174–178
Bristol F.2 Brisfit, 19

Certified engines (*see* Engines, certified)
Classic aircraft, 15, 17–20, 22, 139–148

Climb-out, 35
Constant-speed propellers, 34, 35
Construction books and manuals, 174–178
Construction costs, 8, 21, 34, 139, 179
Construction kits, 4, 7, 33, 109, 144, 203
Construction materials (*see entries beginning with term:*
    Materials)
Construction plans, 11, 26, 32, 37–38, 142–144
    (*See also* Aircraft designs)
Construction space, 30, 173–174
Construction time, 3, 7–9, 11, 12, 21, 33, 149
Continental engines, 34, 154–158, 165
Corrosion prevention, 187–190
Costs, construction, 8, 21, 34, 139, 179
Cowlings, 39, 199
Cox, Jack, 15
Curtiss June Bug replica, 139–141
Curtiss Museum (Hammondsport, N.Y.), 141
Custom aircraft, 8, 149–152
Cylinder-head temperature gauge, 199

Definitions:
    airframe, 39
    alclad material, 179
    general aviation aircraft, 25
    ultralight aircraft, 7
DeHavilland Tiger Moth, 19
Design considerations, 21, 29–40
    airplane configuration and desired characteristics, 30–31
    airport requirements, 35, 36, 138
    construction costs, 8, 21, 34, 139, 179
    construction materials (*see entries beginning with term:*
        Materials)
    construction space, 30, 173–174
    construction time, 3, 7–9, 11, 12, 21, 33, 149
    engines (*see* Engines)
    fabricated parts or kits available, 4, 7, 33, 109, 144, 203
    flight experience, 23–25, 36, 38, 201
    flying preferences and criteria for selecting design, 29, 138
    handling qualities, 17, 18, 23–24, 36–37, 39
    powerplant (*see* Engines)
    preferred seating capacity, 31–32
    propeller, 34, 35
    (*See also* Aircraft designs)
Designers, 21, 37–38
    (*see also* Aircraft designs)
Direct-drive (Lycoming) engines, 160–163
Dissimilar materials, 182–184

Economics (construction costs), 8, 21, 34, 139, 179
Engines, 7, 24, 33–34, 153–170
    automotive, 24, 34, 165, 168–169

Engines (*Cont.*):
    certified, 34, 153–165
        air-cooled, recommended time between overhaul
            (TBO), 165
        Continental, 34, 154–158, 165
        Lycoming, 34, 158–165
    costs, 33–34
    shock mounts, 153, 170
    uncertified, 7, 34, 153, 165–170
        Chotia 460, 166–167
        Geschwender, 169
        Javelin Ford 140T, 168–169
        other, 169–170
        power package kits, 166
        Rotec power units, 166
        RotorWay RW-100, 167–168
        Soarmaster power pack, 166
Experienced amateur rating (NASAD), 17
Experienced experimenter rating (NASAD), 17
Experimental Aircraft Association (EAA):
    Annual International Convention and Sport Aviation
        Exhibition ("Oshkosh"), 5, 8, 12, 16, 18, 22, 23, 25,
        37, 201
        aircraft types attending, 37
    Antique and Classic Division, 15, 18, 22
    chapters of, 15–16, 24, 32, 37
    insurance policy offered by, 196
    regional gatherings of, 201
    relationship to NASAD, 17
    safety-consciousness of, 23–26
    Sport Aviation magazine, 15, 24, 197, 201

Fabricated parts or kits available, 4, 7, 33, 109, 144,
    203
F.E.8 (Fighting Experimental 8) replica, 142, 143
Federal Aviation Administration (FAA), 17, 18
    airworthiness responsibility and, 201–203
    annual inspection requirement, 202–203
    certification standards for production aircraft perfor-
        mance, 12–13
    FAA certified production aircraft, 25
    FAA certified sailplane kit, 109
    Federal Air Regulation (FAR) Part 23, 4, 29
    possible supervision of ultralights by, 21
    regulations on flight of new homebuilts, 199
    reports of conditions found on new and low-time aircraft,
        197
    ultralight licensing and, 128
Fiberglass, 7, 29, 120, 189
Finishes, 187–191
Fixed-pitch propellers, 34
Fixed wing engines (Lycoming), 158–159
Flight experience, 23–25, 36, 38, 201

Flight safety, 23 –26, 195, 197 –199, 201 –203
Fuel and oil system thread seal and antiseize compound, 187

Geared engine (Lycoming), 163 –164
General aviation aircraft, definition of, 25
Geschwender engines, 169
Gliders (see Sailplanes and gliders)

Handling qualities, 17, 18, 23 –24, 36 –37, 39
Hardware, 11
Heat treating aluminum alloy, 184 –186
Heat treating steel, 182, 186
Helicopters, 106 –108
Hoefelmann, Charles D., 149, 152
Homebuilt aircraft:
    construction costs, 8, 21, 34, 139, 179
    construction literature, 139, 142, 143, 174 –178
    construction materials (see entries beginning with term:
        Materials)
    construction plans, 11, 26, 32, 37 –38, 142 –144
        (See also Aircraft designs)
    construction space, 30, 173 –174
    construction time, 3, 7 –9, 11, 12, 21, 33, 149
    construction tools, 173 –176
    design (see Aircraft designs; Design considerations)
    designers, 21, 37 –38
        (See also Aircraft designs)
    engines (see Engines)
    handling qualities, 17, 18, 23 –24, 36 –37, 39
    homebuilder characteristics, 11 –12
    insurance, 195 –196
    numbers under construction, 4, 20, 21, 24
    numbers flying, 4, 20, 21, 25, 128
    safety, 23 –26, 195, 197 –199, 201 –203
Hydraulic-system thread seal and antiseize compound, 187

Inspection procedures, 197, 201 –203
    preflight inspection, 25, 26, 197 –199, 201 –202
Instrument flight rules (IFR) operation, 35
Instrument landing systems (ILS), 35, 36
Insurance, 195 –196
International Aerobatic Club (IAC), 15, 22
Isolation of materials, 182 –184

Joint sealing, 187 –188

Kits or fabricated parts available, 4, 7, 33, 109, 144, 203

Landing(s), 23, 24
    (See also Airport requirements)
Landing gear (tricycle), 36
Landplanes, 40 –105
Literature, aircraft and aircraft construction, 139, 142, 143, 174 –178
Lycoming engines, 34, 158 –165

Materials, 6, 7, 11, 13, 29, 32 –33, 144, 179 –191
    all-metal construction, 29, 32 –33, 120, 174, 179,
        183 –184, 187, 189
    alloys: aluminum, 7, 179 –182, 184 –186
        steel, 180 –182, 186
    alteration or substitution of materials or designs, 24, 25
    construction books and manuals, 174 –178
    dissimilar materials, 182 –184
    fiberglass, 7, 29, 120, 189
    finishes, 187 –190
    hardware, 11
    processes (see Processes)
    sources for, 190 –191
    tools, 173 –176
    wooden construction, 29, 32 –33, 120, 179
Materials hardness, 181
Materials properties, 181, 182
Materials specifications, 180
Materials strength, 179, 181 –183
Museums:
    Curtiss (Hammondsport, N.Y.), 141
    National Air and Space Museum
        (Washington, D. C.), 142
    Owls Head Museum of Transportation (Maine), 141, 142

National Air and Space Museum (Washington, D. C.), 142
National Association of Sport Aircraft Designers (NASAD), 15, 17, 22

Oil and fuel system thread seal and antiseize compound, 187
Oshkosh convention and exhibition, 5, 8, 12, 16, 18, 22, 23, 25, 37, 201
    aircraft types attending, 37
Owls Head Museum of Transportation (Maine), 141, 142

Painting, 187 –191
Parachute, 199
Personal aircraft category, 25
Pioneer aircraft, 139 –148
Pitot, heated, 36

Plans, construction, 11, 26, 32, 37 –38, 142 –144
    (*See also* Aircraft designs)
Poberezny, Paul H., 15, 202
Poberezny, Thomas, 15, 195
Power loading, 35, 36
Powerplant (*see* Engines)
Preflight inspection, 25, 26, 197 –199, 201 –202
Processes, 183 –187
    aluminum alloy heat treat procedures, 184 –187
    application of fuel and oil system thread seal and an-
        tiseize compound, 187
    application of hydraulic-system thread seal and antiseize
        compound, 187
    isolation of dissimilar materials, 182 –184
Propellers, 34, 35

Replica aircraft, 139 –148
Rockwell hardness, 181, 182
Runways, 35, 36, 138

Safety record, 23 –26, 195, 197 –199, 201 –203
Sailplanes and gliders, 20, 109 –119, 144
Schatzie, 149 –152
Sealing threads:
    fuel and oil system, 187
    hydraulic system, 187
Seaplane Pilots Association, 8
Seaplanes, 35, 39, 120 –127
    corrosion prevention, 189 –190
Shock mounts (engine), 153, 170
Shop requirements, 173 –178
Shop tools, 173 –176
Short-coupled aircraft, 23
Short takeoff and landing (STOL) performance, 35
Shoulder harnesses, 199

Skycraft Scout, 21
Spad XIII replica, 142
Sport Aviation magazine, 15, 24, 195, 201
Sprinter, 23
Stearman N2S, 18
Steel and steel alloys, 180 –182, 186
Surface preparation, 187 –188
Surplus parts, 13

Tables:
    aircraft engines, 154 –165
    aircraft types at Oshkosh convention, 37
    materials, comparative properties of, 181
    materials hardness, 181
    materials specifications, 180
Takeoff, pilot skill during, 23
Taube replica, 141 –142
Threaded surfaces, 187
Time between overhaul (TBO) on certified air-cooled en-
        gines, 165
Tooling, 11
Tools, 173 –176
Tricycle landing gear, 36
Troublemakers in new airplanes, 197 –198

Ultralights, 7, 21, 128 –137
Uncertified engines (*see* Engines, uncertified)

Vertical engine (Lycoming), 164

Warbirds of America, 15
Wing loading, 35, 36
Wooden construction, 29, 32 –33, 120, 179
World War II aircraft, 17, 18